AT MY MOTHER'S KNEE

Bridget Boland

At My Mother's Knee

THE BODLEY HEAD

LONDON SYDNEY

TORONTO

British Library Cataloguing
in Publication Data
Boland, Bridget
At my mother's knee.
1 Boland, Bridget 2. Great Britain
– Biography I. Title
941.082'092'4

ISBN 0-370-30145-5

Printed in Great Britain for
The Bodley Head Ltd
9 Bow Street, London WC2E 7AL
by W & J Mackay Limited, Chatham
Set in 'Monotype' Ehrhardt
First published 1978

CONTENTS

ILLUSTRATIONS

FOREWORD

I started to write this book because I had heard part of a discussion on the radio between parents and experts on what to do with the children during what (it seemed) was the tiresome length of the summer holidays. All the advice took the form of how to keep them quiet, and I remembered my mother's reaction to an advertisement for a toy which would 'keep the children quiet for hours'. 'It would keep them quieter still,' she said with disgust, 'just to knock them on the head.' I began a piece I hoped I might read on the radio about my mother's ways with her six children, and found that I had far too much to say. To explain her attitudes I would have to put in a good deal about her own eccentric upbringing in contrast to ours; and then I came to realise that I was the product of all the childhoods of those closest to me. The result is an interwoven tapestry of all their influences.

B.B.

My Mother

My mother's main object in life, so far as her children were concerned, was to see that we reaped the benefits of her own childhood without suffering the disadvantages. It was not that she had
been poor, or unhappy; but she had had, to all intents and purposes, no home, and she had been quite dreadfully lonely. An
only child herself, she was determined that there should be a great
many of us to keep each other company. She achieved six of us,
over a period of twenty years ('which had the disadvantage that
there was always someone in the house having measles or whoop-
ing-cough'). She was also determined that we should have a home,
somewhere to put down roots, geographically as well as emotion-
ally. This she achieved too. Indeed she succeeded too well: the
habit of taking root, once acquired, is hard to lose. When I was
grown up, I once had six weeks to spare and £25 to spend (it was
just after the War), and I decided to see Provence, starting at
Avignon. Six weeks and £25 later I was still in Avignon. I went
to Rome to work on a film for a couple of months, and twelve
years later I was still in Rome.

She was born in Australia, in 1876, and both sides of her
family, the Moloneys and the Quirks, had certainly had roots
there, being among the earliest settlers. It was her grandfather
Patrick Moloney who had organised the inhabitants of Melbourne
into patrolling the beach with guns to hold off the first convict

ship which arrived—intending to start a penal settlement there like the one in New South Wales. They induced it to go on to Tasmania, and no penal settlement was ever established in Victoria. Much of what is now Melbourne was built on Moloney farmland, and the site of the Quirk house, Carlton, 'a palace in the Bush', is now the suburb of that name. My mother had many stories of the early settlers: of John Fawkner, the explorer who opened up the interior, who reached civilisation again, literally crawling up the steps, at the Carlton house; of Ned Kelly, of the famous Kelly Gang who wore iron masks, whose sister was a maid at the house; of the day when her grandmother had driven into the city in the morning passing 'Canvas Town', now the suburb of Fitzroy but then made up of the tents of prospectors, and found driving home in the evening that the whole lot had vanished: the Gold Rush had started.

But both families were Irish, always spoke of Ireland as home, sent their sons to school at Stonyhurst so that they could spend their holidays in Ireland, and went back and forth to visit them. Distances never seem to have had much significance for them.

At the age of eight my mother was brought to England for the first time. There had been a long drought in Victoria. Rain had been described to her as being like the contents of a watering can pouring from the sky, so that did not surprise her too much; but though she had seen pictures of snow it had never occurred to her that it made no sound. They went first to the Lake District, because of her father's abiding passion for the Lake Poets, and when she first saw a blizzard of great white flakes falling in dead silence she went off into terrified hysterics.

She had had a geography book in the nursery which stated categorically that 'in Australia the flowers have no scent and the birds have no song', and had thereafter decided that 'the only thing to do was to go to places yourself'. To places she certainly went. From the convent boarding school in Roehampton, to which she was now sent, she always (apart from an occasional trip to Australia) spent the holidays with her parents wherever in Europe they might be. They lived an entirely nomadic existence, moving from hotel to hotel. Her father ('Gran's husband', as we called the tall, impressive, bearded figure in the photographs at home, for we had never known him) had qualified as both a barrister and a doctor with a view to becoming an expert in forensic medicine; but he did not practise long in either capacity. Money was luckily no object, and he lavished all his time on a passionate enjoyment of art.

Occasionally my mother found another child staying in a hotel to play with, but soon either the child or my mother would be moved on. In those days people who travelled for pleasure seldom took their children with them, they left them at home, or sent them to rented accommodation at the seaside, with nurses or governesses.

My grandmother was going blind. 'Woman,' exclaimed her husband as their carriage from Posillipo drove round the Bay of Naples, 'how dare you knit in the face of Nature!' She was trying not to let him or their child know how little she could see. I have difficulty in imagining her in those days. When I knew her she had immense personality, tall and alarming and delighting in shocking us. She used to bounce my youngest sister about, singing:

> 'Oh, my sister Anne
> Has an arm like a man,
> And a damn fine leg for a stocking',

and once when I was telling what I thought a most romantic story about the mother of a friend of mine who had never taken off her wedding ring since the day she was married, Gran snatched off her own ring crying 'Away, you bauble!' and tossed it over her shoulder into the dining-room fireplace. I know that my mother when small was convinced that she was nothing but a disappointment to her, for she had once heard two grown-ups discussing her. 'Poor woman,' one had said, 'she so longed for a boy, and there's only the one little girl.' She certainly found her father the more congenial companion.

She adored him, and went with him everywhere he would take her; and where he took her was 'to see things', particularly in art galleries and churches. He would march round a piece of sculpture, she told me, rhapsodising over its anatomical perfections, brandishing his walking stick to point them out, to the alarm of attendants on duty who would follow him nervously from piece to piece. Then he would suddenly demand a chair, or even, if the piece was large enough, a ladder; he had a passion for ears. He had once alarmed Nellie Melba at dinner by staring fixedly at her ear all the evening, tilting his chair back to continue to examine it when she turned her head to speak to him: he had a theory that 'an ear for music' started in the outer whorls of its structure. He also had a theory that ears revealed criminal tendencies, and that those of statues showed that sculptors had used members of the criminal classes as models. 'He's really quite safe,' my mother would whisper to an attendant, and coax him into bringing a chair for Papa to stand on, so long as the stick was left on the ground.

Her parents both had infinite charm. On one occasion, before she was born, they had been wandering about Europe when their funds ran out. Their money was in a family trust, and the trustees, considering that it was time they settled down, took the drastic measure of cutting off supplies. My grandmother, going to Mass at Notre Dame in Paris, left her purse with the last of their cash on her seat when she went to Communion, and it was stolen. They told their hotel of their predicament, and the management were so distressed for them that they not only refrained from pressing for their bills to be paid but lent them enough money 'to enjoy Paris' until their trustees should see the light, or give up hope. On another occasion, a Swiss hotel left a nought off a bill by mistake. My grandfather paid it blithely without noticing, but my grandmother, asking (she could not by then see to read) what their stay had cost, realised the discrepancy and sent the difference. The following year, back at the same hotel, my mother got measles very badly, and was put in a detached chalet with a nurse and, of course, a great deal of extra service for several weeks. When they were due to leave it was found that no extra—not even the room for the nurse—had been charged. My grandmother protested that they really didn't know their own silly business, but the management stuck to their guns: it was a delight to serve such people, and they wouldn't dream of profiting from the dear little girl's illness. Hotels in those days, as well as my grandparents, must have had considerable charm.

In one respect at least travellers on the continent at that time were better off than we are; they could visit private art collections freely. Although some, like the Colonna and Doria galleries in Rome, are now open to the public, as so many are in England, most are not; and you would get a very chilly reception nowadays if you simply rang the doorbell and asked to see the family treasures. In the 18th century, gentlemen making the Grand Tour had taken it for granted that they should see all the best of whatever any country possessed. They carried, of course, letters of introduction to many great folk on their route; but the lack of a note to the owner never bothered Horace Walpole, for instance, if there was a picture or statue that he wanted to see. My grandfather maintained this robust tradition, considering that all works of art were to that extent in the public domain, and that anyone but a barbarian would recognise the fact and be delighted to show any they possessed. Even if he knew nothing of a house's treasures but merely took a fancy to its architecture he would invade it. Driving along a country road he would see a castle, perhaps, and with my mother in tow would get out and march up to the door. If there was no answer to the bell he would rap on the door with his blackthorn, and ask whoever opened it if the owner would graciously allow him to visit the private chapel which, he had heard, was of great beauty. 'There's always a chapel,' he explained to my mother, 'and people like to think it's been heard of.' Once inside, and lavishing knowledgeable enthusiasm on everything, he would end by being shown 'from turrets to dungeons', often finding things that were in no guidebooks or local histories, of whose worth even the owners might know nothing. He had no lust to own such things himself. 'What, and lug them about?' he asked. He looked, as other people eat, and having feasted his eyes moved on, after duly tipping the housekeeper after the manner of the Grand Tour.

It was not only great houses that would take his fancy. Once, seeing a German woodcarver at his bench through an open doorway, he rapped on the back of it and strode in, spending several hours studying the man at work, making sketches of his tools (comparing them later with their mediaeval equivalents and finding little difference), while my mother sat on a stool and made a doll out of curly woodshavings from the floor.

Above all, though, she came to know the great galleries of Europe as well as any guide, and she felt that she could give us at least the galleries of London in the same way.

I was eight when she first took me into the National Gallery. Just before we reached the top of the stairs she told me to close my eyes and take her hand. We lived quite near the National and even nearer to the Tate Gallery, but always until now to go inside was a treat promised for 'when you're old enough'. The only 'real' pictures we had at home were portraits of my mother and her three older children, and we were always told that the Medici prints and the reproductions in books that we had were 'nothing like the real thing', which in those days of poor colour processes was indeed true. The moment when each child was old enough to enjoy the real thing was carefully gauged.

I would not for the world have peeked and spoiled the surprise as my mother led me by the hand. The pictures would be much, much larger than the prints and reproductions, of course, and, I supposed, much softer-looking, for the 'real' portraits of us at home were in a mixture of pastel and tempera fashionably considered suitable for pictures of children at the time. But when my mother told me I could open my eyes we were in a wonderland of jewel-bright colours, with story-book people in glorious clothes living in castles and houses with arches and pillars and splendid hangings, with views through the windows of more castles and fascinating little uphill streets of more story-book houses, with little bright people hurrying about. I was enchanted, and hurried from one Flemish, French or Italian primitive to another. They were best, of course, if you knew the story, and here was a Nativity, for instance, but how much brighter and more exciting than the crib that was brought out every Christmas at home, with the colours of its little old Italian figures darkened by much handling over the years. There in the picture was a procession coming: that had to be the Three Kings. At home we always ceremoniously took out the King figures from their tissue paper and installed them on the Epiphany, and here in another picture the Kings had already arrived; and such Kings, with such gorgeous embroidered robes, such bejewelled golden crowns! 'Here are some more Kings over here,' said my mother. 'Which do you like best?'

I have no idea how long we spent that first day among those very early paintings, except that it was not nearly long enough when my mother said: 'Now close your eyes again,' and led me away. When I was told to open them it was like being plunged into icy water. We were standing in front of a huge picture all black and white, a father and mother in black with huge white ruffs and children all in black and white too, except for their rosy cheeks. After all those glorious colours and busy, gay people in their wonderful world, the still solemnity of that worthy Dutch 17th century family was a shock that left me speechless. I stared for a long time. 'But,' I said at last, 'I do rather like it, too.'

'Thank God,' said my mother. 'That's enough for today.' She whisked me out, and as a further treat to mark the occasion we went home in a taxi.

Going round galleries with her father had been fun, and fun, above all, it must be for us; so first we looked mostly at 'story' subjects, while she told us the stories (religious, mythological or historical) that we didn't know. Then she would ask, perhaps, pretending that she couldn't remember, where we had seen the same story pictured before, and then go back to that room and look at it again, seeing how differently each painter saw the story. Sometimes we could go back to two or three rooms, and compare, and decide who told the story best. The first time I recognised a story and exactly where to look for another version of it for myself (alas, I can't remember what it was) my mother said, 'Hooray! Now let's start looking for something else.'

What came next? I think it was 'places', looking particularly at the kind of places different painters chose to make the stories happen in, from the busy little mediaeval towns of my first loves, the primitives, through classical settings, to romantic landscapes. From that we started looking for the way the landscapes were shown. There was an exciting day when we first had another doting look at the glimpses out of the windows of my beloved primitives in the National and then ('Remember them—hold on to

My mother, 1884

Bridget, 1914

ENGAGEMENT PORTRAITS
My mother's parents, c. 1874
My parents, 1901

them') whisked in a taxi down to the Tate, and I was given my
first sight of my mother's favourite Turner. On that occasion at
least the shock effect was certainly achieved again. And I remember we walked home along the Embankment and my mother
told me that before I was born she used to walk and walk there,
soaking up sky and river, in case what they said about 'pre-natal
influences' was true and she could implant delight in them in my
unborn mind.

'I really believe perhaps you're old enough to play Gallia
now,' she said one day. 'Gallia', as we called it, was the best card
game ever invented. In spite of repeated requests from various
members of my family to the National Gallery over the last fifty
years, it can no longer be played, so far as I know, except by anyone who cares to at my house. The first duty that was impressed
by the rest of us on each of my sisters when they married was to
write to the Gallery in their new names and from their new
addresses (in case they had a file under 'Boland', labelled 'mono-
maniacs—answer as before') and demand that they re-issue the
game. It consists of fifty-six cards. Thirteen of them are 'guide
cards', giving the name of an English painter (with his dates and a
couple of lines of biography) and the titles of a number of his
paintings in the national collections, with the date and a few
words about each. The other cards are each a photographic
reproduction of a painting with nothing else but the title. The
game is played like Happy Families, the object being to collect
all the works of a painter to make a 'family'. If you have a guide
card it is easy; you say 'So-and-so, please may I have The Valley
Farm by Constable.' If you have The Valley Farm and you can't
remember or guess rightly who painted it and have not the
appropriate guide card to identify it by, you have to wait till
someone else asks for it with the name of the painter attached. If
you guess and ask for what you hope is the right guide card and

have guessed wrongly, you have to give back the guide card, and miss a turn. When the players are really skilled the guide cards can be removed from the pack, and held in reserve for reference when heated arguments arise.

My mother detested card games—oh, all those terrible long evenings in all those hotels when she had watched her mother, while her sight was good enough, being forced from good nature to make a fourth yet again at Bridge, which she loathed; and oh! those kindly grown-ups who used to offer to play cards with the lonely little girl and considered that 'no, thank-you' was only shyness to be jovially overridden. I have no idea whether she hated Gallia as she did other cards, but she would play it forever whenever asked. As the years went by great English paintings developed irreverent nick-names: The 'View at Hampstead' became 'The Mucky Sky by Turner, please', 'Sigismonda Mourning over the Heart of Guiscardo' by Hogarth was 'Sigith'. Visitors to the Tate were surprised by one of us, who had watched while too young to play, suddenly shouting 'Mummy, Mummy, look—there's Ekky Ank!' and pointing to Ecce Ancilla Domini by Rossetti.

Above all, my mother always encouraged you to like whatever picture *you* liked, and was immensely interested to hear why you liked it, and could always see just what you meant; and it would remind her of another picture by the same painter or of the same subject somewhere else, and we would go off to some other gallery to see it. I had a blind spot: the French Impressionists at the Tate, particularly Seurat's 'Bathers in the Seine', which she loved and I thought flat, colourless and plain ugly. She didn't force them on me, but drew me out on what I didn't like about them (thereby, of course, causing me to look at them for longer). 'It's as if they couldn't see properly,' I objected, 'Why didn't they get glasses?' It wasn't till some forty years later that I read

Patrick Trevor Roper's *World Through Blunted Sight*, and was pleased to find that my diagnosis had been correct, but then was startled to see, in quotations from Monet and Renoir, the gist of what my mother had answered me: 'Perhaps they tried glasses and liked the world better without them.'

Everything about children fascinated my mother. Perhaps we represented all the children she had never had to play with in all those months and years of hotel-bound holidays. Her mind was completely open, she had no preconceived ideas about what children were or ought to be like, and was forever discovering and re-discovering the exciting fact (as she told me when I was older) that each was completely different. Her attempts to interest or amuse us were always tentative. My eldest sister and my brother had not particularly cared about pictures (except when playing Gallia), and she had found the charms of gallery-visiting quickly exhausted and had therefore dropped it, tried again when they were older, and dropped it again. Maureen, four years older than I, and Eily, four years younger, couldn't have enough of it. Of all of us, only Anne, ten years younger than I, had any creative artistic talent herself; it showed itself early, and was gleefully encouraged at home; and yet, to my mother's excited fascination, Anne of all of us took the least interest in looking at pictures by other people. 'You wait,' my mother said to me, 'the best pictures for her are in her own head.'

Because each child was different, and at each age was at a different stage of development, we each when young always went alone with her to galleries so that she could concentrate on what would give each the most pleasure. My own abiding passion for mediaeval paintings led her early to take me to the British Museum displays of illuminated manuscripts, where I could dote on the enchanting little pictures that adorned them. This seemed to her natural enough; but when we went to the Tate, the fact that I fell in love as soon as I was shown them (some time later) with Rossetti and company astonished her. She did not care for them at all herself. She told me later that she had been excited then to realise suddenly what I saw in them. 'You'd never heard of Pre-Raphaelitism, but obviously you were seeing what they had in common with your primitives. To my eye it was all overlaid with Victorian romanticism, but when you fastened with delight on the precision of details in some flowers in the grass, the pattern of a damask robe, I wanted to ring up heaven and get poor Rossetti on the line and tell him he *had* pulled it off after all, to the seeing eye of a child.'

She treasured all the 'discovery' remarks we made, such as Maureen's (who loved landscapes of any period) on looking at a Claude: 'I like it when they paint the air—that one smells of mist in it,' and my own on first seeing Van Gogh's Chair in the Tate: 'It's frightening. He's mad!' I think it was because she listened every bit as much as she talked when you looked at pictures with her that gallery-going never struck me as an educational exercise: it was a shared joyous experience, like going to a circus.

One game, my favourite, that we used to play in galleries or with her books and postcards at home was called 'going for a walk in a picture'. This also was developed from her own lonely girlhood abroad. By the time she was fourteen or so, my grandmother was almost completely blind, but still trekked from hotel to hotel in the wake of her ever-travelling husband, with my mother in tow. 'Gran's husband' had always been an enthusiastic sampler of the wines of the country, of all wines of all countries. By middle age, when perhaps the feeling that he had never done anything with his life except enjoy it began to depress him, he was drinking very heavily indeed—so heavily that there had been 'scenes' in most of the best hotels in Europe. Although, as I have indicated, all hoteliers loved and pitied my grandmother, and indeed liked her husband, whose personality was enchanting, returning to hotels where there had been 'scenes' the year before became embarrassing, so they would go to the second-best the next time round. But the second-best were not, naturally enough, as good as the best; gran's husband would all the sooner feel the urge to move on elsewhere, and the pace became faster, and my mother could make even fewer friends.

She had friends, of course, at school—she adored school; but because of the nature of her cosmopolitan hotel life in the holidays, and such companionship as she had being with older people, she was older and more sophisticated for her age than most of her contemporaries. The convent belonged to a French order which had houses in all the capitals of the world, and it was extremely convenient for Catholic diplomats of all countries to send their children there. It was at Roehampton, then just outside London, and the children could be easily visited, and when the parents were moved to another *poste* the children would simply be moved to the house of the same order in the new capital and take up their education, which was the same in all, exactly where they had left off in England. My mother was never conscious of learning languages, she acquired them as she moved about; she spoke French and Italian as well as she spoke English, and German and Spanish very nearly as well. She had enough Portuguese 'for practical purposes', and 'anyone who can speak English and German can speak Dutch.' The foreign children at Roehampton tended to have seen more of the world than the English ones, and to them she gravitated. She never had an English friend close enough to invite her home in the holidays. But the foreign children were the ones who, like those she met in hotels abroad, tended to be moved on, so that here, too, her friendships were mostly fleeting. And now, in the holidays, she was seeing less of her father because he was drinking more, and she was thrown more and more on her own resources.

The only places where, in those days, a young girl could go with propriety alone were to church and to picture galleries. My grandmother travelled without a maid, and there was no-one to send my mother out with after a few abortive attempts at finding holiday governesses who would fit the peculiar bill had failed. So to churches (more about that later) and to galleries and museums, my mother went. When her father went with her to one of the latter he would find some fatherly-looking attendant, tip him lavishly, and ask him to see that if she came in alone she was not 'troubled' by anyone, and tip him again, next time he went in himself, to keep up the good work. This had its drawbacks, for sometimes pleasant visitors to a gallery, native or foreign, would be disposed to get into conversation with the lonely-looking young girl, and be scared off by an officious attendant, earning his tip or over-conscious of his duty, who would whisper that Mademoiselle —the Signorina—the Fraülein—had been committed to his care by Milord her Papa (all English gentlemen abroad were still Milords in those days). On one occasion my mother, at about sixteen, was hugely amused to overhear one attendant solemnly warning the perfectly respectable but perhaps too young and good-looking father of two children, who had got into conversation with her, that Milord her Papa, well-known amateur of the arts, was an immense man, over six foot high (as indeed was the case), well-known also as an eccentric much given to flourishing 'a walking stick with knobs all the way up' (his favourite blackthorn). The information, retailed when she got back to the hotel, delighted her father, and the officious attendant was no doubt more heavily tipped than ever, and he was always careful that it was his blackthorn that he carried when introducing her to a new gallery.

Now that my mother had seen much of Europe she began to

recognise, during the hours she spent looking at pictures, buildings and corners of streets and squares that she knew incorporated in the paintings. She began to collect postcards everywhere she went, the better to identify such originals. We still had those postcards at home, and when we were going to see a certain picture she would take the appropriate ones with her and show me how an artist had incorporated such a tower or dome or archway in Rome or Florence, Padua or Milan, in his concept of Jerusalem, or such a street in Antwerp or Bruges out of a window in his painting of an interior. Or we would find a reproduction of the painting in one of her books, and hunt through albums of postcards till we identified it. This led on to our playing the game she had invented for herself of walking into the canvas and reconstructing if we knew, or imagining if we didn't, what would be round the next corner, just out of sight in the painting. The pictures became three-dimensional, you could walk about in them for ages. As I came to know more about the kind of houses people lived in at different times, we would walk in through open doorways, too, and discuss what the rooms would be like, what the people would be doing, whether there would be a courtyard at the back, would it have a pump, or a fountain, or even a little paved garden like the one in such-and-such another painting. Long drives in hired carriages out into the country with her parents from their hotels had given her a knowledge of the landscapes painters would have known, particularly in Tuscany, Umbria, and round Paris and in the Loire valley; and she would tell me how the hills in the background of a crucifixion by Perugino were near so-and-so, and we would go home and find them, perhaps, on a postcard or in a travel book, and thereafter be able to walk for miles through Perugino's little humpy hills.

It never occurred to me for an instant that I was learning a good deal about other things besides paintings from all this: about architecture, and geography, and social life, and costume and furniture, and weapons and armour and even the development of cooking utensils. The fun of the game was to know exactly what to 'see' inside those houses or round those corners that would fit with the rest of the picture, to chase off to some other remembered picture and see whether this or that seen in it could indeed fairly be included (because the costume in both was of the same period, or the artist had known the same town or countryside). At first she and I played it together, then when I was old enough I could join my mother when she played it with Maureen, and when Eily was old enough she could join my mother and me.

Such games as these and 'guess the painter' or 'guess the date', other people must have played in galleries, but there was one which I am sure was unique to our family. It was called 'Saints'.

My mother, in her visits to churches wherever she went, had of course always looked at the paintings and sculpture. Her father, when he went with her, was always interested in the work of art itself and its contents rather than its subject. Once, when he was admiring the superb accuracy of veins and arthritic limbs in a picture of an aged man, my mother, then very young, had asked him, 'But how do you know it's Saint Jerome?' They were in a church, not a gallery, and there was no title under the painting. 'Because he's an old hermit living in a cave and he's got a tame lion, but look at the swollen knuckles of that left hand. He gets a lot of pain, poor old boy.' It was the fact that the presence of a tame lion made it St Jerome that intrigued my mother, and she wanted to know more about that. She got St Jerome's story, and those of most other saints, from her mother.

Gradually she discovered (largely with the aid of Mrs Jameson's *Sacred and Legendary Art*) how to recognise practically every saint in the canon by his or her symbol (usually drawn from some legend of his life or martyrdom): St Catherine of Alexandria would have a spiked wheel at her side and often a sword in her hand (they failed to liquidate her by rolling her down hill bound to a wheel, and had to finish her off with a sword); St Catherine of Siena would hold or wear a ring (she had a vision in which she became the Bride of Christ); St Barbara would have a miniature tower as a symbol of her imprisonment; two young men dressed as doctors with scarlet robes and caps would be St Cosmos and St Damian, and a deacon with a gridiron would be St Laurence who was burned to death on one (remarking, so my mother said, 'You can turn me over now, I'm done on this side'); and so on.

She found that this did not only apply to the patron of a church. A guide book would tell her that a certain side chapel had been decorated for a local Guild—of doctors say (and there sure enough would be a picture of two young men in the approved scarlet robes and caps, Sts Cosmos and Damian, patrons of the Guild), or of Carpenters (and there would be St Joseph with his lily). If the guide book said nothing, and in the side chapel there was St Barbara with her tower, my mother would be able to guess that it was the chapel of the local artillerymen's Guild, of which she was the patron, or that perhaps it had been decorated at the expense of the whole town to celebrate the end of a siege. She could then in imagination fill the little chapel with robed apothecaries, or craftsmen, or armoured gunners, on their saint's day, and bring the empty church alive.

In London, Cromwell and such had knocked everything about too much and such few old churches as there were were mostly filled only with what my mother lumped together as 'dead protestants'. In the summer we lived in a fishing village in northern France, where there was only one statue of a patron, known as St Wilgefort, a character with a full skirt and tight bodice but indeterminate shape below it, tied to a cross, with a beard but generally accepted as a female, about whom even my mother could find out nothing at all.

My mother had developed the game further in her own girl-hood when she found out about 'donors'. These, she explained, were the people who had donated a picture to a church, and whose Christian names, at any rate, could often be identified by saints shown in the picture. Say there was a Madonna and Child in the middle with a number of saints, and a man kneeling on the right-hand side of the picture, and perhaps a woman kneeling on the other, with sometimes children kneeling as well, the boys behind their fathers and the girls behind their mothers. If the saint on the right nearest the central figures was a bishop, say, carrying three small bags or gold balls, he would be St Nicholas, name-saint of the man kneeling in the foreground. The nearest woman saint to the central figures on the other side would be the patroness of the wife of the donor—St Lucy perhaps, with two eyes on a plate, or St Agatha, with two breasts on a dish, symbols of their martyrdoms, though both with the full quota of eyes and breasts in the normal places (as they would have them, 'of course', in heaven). The second saint on the right might be the patron of the church to which the picture was donated, or of the town, or of a guild of which the donor was master—and so on. If there were exactly as many extra saints as there were children, I used to prefer to think they were the name-saints of the children them-selves. You began to feel so much closer a relationship to the picture when you knew so much about it.

A kindly German professor who met my mother in a hotel in Florence and discovered this interest of hers, added to it with the gift of beautifully copied drawings from a book of his: the coats of arms of popes and of great families all over Italy. He explained to her how you could often date a building or a picture by the arms of a pope on it (unless it were a Medici pope, for instance, because there were several). She could sometimes add the sur-

name to the Christian name of a donor if she looked carefully for
a coat of arms somewhere in the picture, in a stained glass window
in the background, perhaps, or a symbol from it carved on the
Madonna's throne or woven into the damask or brocade of her
robe—or of the donor's own. Many years later, my mother, my
sister Maureen and I were in Bruges in 1930, the centenary of the
Belgian kingdom. In celebration of it a temporary museum had
been erected, an enormous conglomeration of rather Nissen-hut
affairs, the most beautiful gallery I have ever seen. The walls were
hung with light grey velvet, on which, all at eye level, were hung
all the great Flemish masterpieces from the private collections of
the families of the province. At the same time was published, for a
pageant to be held in the city, a booklet that gave the arms of all
these old families, who were to send floats to the pageant. Never
did we play such a splendid version of the 'Saints' game: dis-
regarding the description the catalogue provided, we could work
out Christian and surnames to our hearts' content. What I particularly liked were the wedding chests occasionally placed in a
corner with wonderful paintings inset as panels: I could identify,
from saints and family symbols, the name of the bride. It was
almost like knowing her, and being invited to the wedding. One
morning Maureen and I went into this temporary gallery just
after it opened, and were appalled to see a nice young man in
overalls with a bucket of soapy water and a sponge, whistling as
he gave every picture a nice freshening up for the day. Surely the
water would soak through the paint and rot the wood on which
most of them were painted? We weren't sure enough to protest,
and, as Maureen said, he was such a nice cheerful young man,
who had greeted us politely in both Flemish and French (which in
that militantly Flemish part of Belgium at that time was a polite-
ness indeed). We hurried back to our hotel and told my mother.

'It's almost impossible to damage really old paint,' she said, 'but you're right about the panel. Oh! for father's blackthorn, I'd go and hit the director over the head with it, and I haven't so much as an umbrella! I'll go and tell him how much we've all enjoyed the gallery and ask him to lunch, and drop it into the conversation by the way.'

Gran's husband had been very interested in painting techniques, and had conveyed to my mother a good deal of haphazard information on the subject from which she had gone on to discover more. It was the one thing about pictures in which she could never interest any of us, even Anne, who was going to be the artist of the family. True to her principle of never forcing information for which one wasn't ready, when she found that I positively disliked 'knowing how it was done', she gave up. The crux came when she was showing me how a pointilliste painting was built up of dots of colour like a mosaic. I said, 'Ugh, think of the horrid little man going spot, spot, spot, like giving the poor landscape measles! The only result is you have to go almost out into the street to see what the picture's supposed to be of, anyway.' To me, paintings were real: real places, real people. I hated the idea of the painter's vision having to be re-created by tedious fiddling mechanics, it spoilt the magic. Yet years and years later when picture cleaning and restoration became my hobby and I had to learn about techniques, even from this area where she had failed to interest me and quickly stopped, I used to hear echoes of things she had said: how the jewel-brightness of the early paintings I loved was achieved by painting layer after layer of the same colour very thinly one on top of the other, 'sort of trapping the light in between the layers to make them glow'; and, 'Look how Claude paints a tiny brown cross on the white in the middle of his golden sun—it makes it spin, that's what dazzles.' It must have sunk into my subconscious, but at the time what she showed me was the sun itself.

My Father

My mother said she believed firmly in the descent of my father's family (like that of all other Irish families) from the ancient Kings. 'The poor fellows can have had no subjects,' objected my father, 'except their own too-many offspring.'

'But,' said my mother, turning my youngest sister to him for inspection, 'look at this child's knees! They were washed half an hour ago, and she has done nothing since but sit here with me. She has subcutaneous glands in them that ooze dirt.'

'Ah, well,' said my father, 'I dare say she comes by them honestly, then.' It was then explained to me that the original Boland (Beolain, pronounced Beolawn and meaning Little Mouth) was the son of Nial Black Knee, son of Nial of the Nine Hostages (we were up to no good, evidently, long before the English came to give us an excuse). The same ancestry, she held, explained why all her children had mouths too small for the normal complement of teeth, and had to have them widened with elaborate, painful, and extremely expensive plates.

Mythology apart, my father was born in 1870, and christened John Pius to console Pope Pius IX for the loss of the Papal States. He was even known as Pius at home until, suffering agonies at school in England from his brother giving this shameful fact away, he fined each of his relations sixpence every time they failed to call him John. Their parents both dying when their seven children were very young, the family were brought up by their guardian, uncle on their mother's side, who was Assistant Bishop of Dublin, making a strange household for a Catholic prelate. Even their family jokes had an ecclesiastical flavour, a particularly good one, my father told me, being awarded a 'pontifical high laugh' of three times three, from the fact that a High Mass in the presence of a bishop has three priests at the altar.

His childhood must have been nearly as different from my mother's as mine was to be. The two boys and five girls lived in Dublin with their uncle and the lady known to my generation as Granny Dilly, a remote cousin called Adda Dillon, who came to look after them. She brought the girls up in such 'innocence' that at least one of them honestly did not know when she married that her new state meant any more than going to live in the country with her husband instead of in Dublin with her uncle, and was deeply shocked by her honeymoon.

The family was very much a family. Except that the two boys went to school in England and the girls had governesses at home, they went everywhere *en bloc*, migrating in the summer to a sprawling house in County Wicklow at first and then to another on Rosdohan Island where my father fell in love forever with County Kerry. Whether they cruised round the Mediterranean or to Australia, or went to see the Passion Play at Oberammergau, the whole tribe moved together like locusts. My mother used to say that with such a horde of Bolands surging about it was odd that on her own travels she never bumped into them for so long. Finally, with his brother Patrick, a year older, my father went for a year to Bonn University. Nobody, apparently, did anything there but duel, unless they could belong to the exclusive Bavarian Club whose members, as Catholics, were forbidden to duel, and therefore did nothing but drink, and to this the two brothers were fortunately elected. I have a very handsome beer mug, decorated with the club arms and my father's name, and a book of student songs with little metal knobs on all the corners, back and front, so that it could be laid open on a table and not be damaged by the beer swilling about underneath.

My father, when I knew him, did not drink at all. How had he managed, I asked him, at such gatherings? 'Patrick talked,' he said. 'His German was like his French, elegant and witty, he could make exquisite puns, which Germans always find astonishing.' 'But you . . .?' 'Oh, I made friends. And I sang.' A year of this was evidently considered by their uncle the Bishop enough for this stage of their education, and the two proceeded to Oxford, where my father played rugger and cricket for Christ Church and cricket also in minor games for the University, though never against Cambridge. His brother Patrick confined his sporting activities to giving dinners to both teams whenever my father played in any, including the splendid rugger and cricket matches against the men from Catholic schools at Cambridge, for which he managed to find teams from the twenty Catholic undergraduates at Oxford. It was from these occasions that the Newman Societies sprang (Cardinal Newman had been the Bolands' Headmaster at the Oratory School), now established on a deeply serious religious and cultural basis at all English universities. Patrick also studied every subject in sight except Law, which they were both reading, and in which, after taking a private tutor to Jersey for six weeks in their last vacation before their finals for some extensive cramming, they managed to take degrees even if of the lowest possible class.

My father went to Greece to recuperate, where he found the first of the modern Olympic Games (1896) in progress. An Austrian friend from Oxford was competing in the tennis, then included in the games, and his partner in the doubles was ill; so my father partnered him, and they won. Officials ran up the

Austrian flag and the Union Jack. My father objected: the Irish flag, he explained, bore a gold harp on a green ground. They apologised profusely and said that they would have one ready in future; whereat he went on to beat his doubles partner in the finals of the singles. 'Never mind,' said my father to the distressed officials, 'the Union Jack will do to be going on with; but maybe you'd better just have a flag ready with "J. P. Boland" on it, it'll be easier to make. My real forte is putting the shot.' Luckily, however, he was deflected from the rest of the games by a chance to meet Schliemann, the famous archaeologist who had recently excavated Troy; but he always considered that those first games had a blissfully happy atmosphere compared with those when intense national rivalries took over.

I have always found it difficult to equate the John Boland of those days with the father I knew, for by then he had found both his Cause and my mother, and his life was polarised.

But first came the High Romance of St Jean de Luz. The family were staying in that then unpopularised little town when two young Frenchmen who had a house there saw my father and his brother playing tennis on the hotel court, and conceived the idea of getting up a tournament between residents in the district and guests at the hotel. Asking the manager the names of the two visitors that they were watching, they were told it was 'Beaulan'— the way the family always pronounced their name in France. Presuming them French, the two residents introduced themselves as what sounded like 'Haut Birne de St Gery' and proposed their plan. It was not until lists of possible players were hastily jotted down by both sides that the spellings Boland and O'Byrne emerged; and here I must explain about the Wild Geese.

At the time of the Rebellion in England, many Loyalists followed the defeated King James II to France, where they formed Irish regiments in the French army while confidently awaiting a

Patty Dillon, c. 1863

My father, standing centre, with his brother and sisters,
and his uncle (guardian) and cousin (companion), 1893

My mother, aged 16, and her father

Patrick Moloney, 1899

restoration; others fled to Spain where there had been many Irish
since the Flight of the Earls nearly a hundred years earlier, or to
Austria, and formed Irish units there. By 1714 there was a whole
Irish Brigade in the French service, five regiments of foot and two
of horse. The depot of the Brigade was at Bordeaux with a sub-
depot at Marseilles, and recruiting from Ireland continued, ships
going out with French wines and brandy as ballast and (after
dropping off a good many barrels under the guard of the excise
men on the South and West Coasts of England and the re-
mainder in Cork and Kerry) returning with a full complement of recruits for the Brigade, a trade which continued
till the reorganisation of the French Army at the Revolution. By
1829 the Emancipation Act had made it legal for Catholics to hold
commissions in the British army, but by that time generations
of Irish had grown up in France. They had tended to marry, if
not each other's daughters, girls of the Bordeaux and Marseilles
regions, and if the latter were heiresses to local vineyards, well,
there is more than one way of being a mercenary; and some of the
great names in the French wine trade were soon Irish, such as
Hennessey in Cognac and, some say, Haut Brion (O'Brien) in the
claret country. Among them were the O'Byrnes, Counts of St
Gery. Links with Ireland were proudly kept up although the
families might not have set foot there for two hundred years.
When I learned that one of General de Gaulle's ancestresses had
been a MacCarthy of Marseilles (where there is a cemetery full of
such names), I wondered whether some of the difficulties the
General had with Churchill during the war might not have been
consciously atavistic.

The delight of the O'Byrnes and the Bolands with each other
is thus understandable. Adda Dillon of course was with the latter
as chaperone to the girls. Her own younger sister, orphaned at
three years old, had been parcelled up and sent to their cousin

Charles Dillon (pronounced Di'on), a General in the ordinary French army, since Dillon's Irish Regiment was no more. The two families settled down to a romantic interchange of linked genealogies, and Patrick Boland and Eleanore O'Byrne (promptly rechristened Norah) fell madly in love. Her mother, a von Hübner, was Austrian, and this led to the bringing in of the Irish-Austrian connection, notably the O'Kellys. It was decided that for the wedding of Patrick and Norah the following year there should be a *grande réunion de famille* of every remotely connected descendant of the Wild Geese who could be summoned from anywhere in Europe to St Jean de Luz. In the heightened romance of this occasion, everyone promptly fell in love with everyone else, O'Byrnes and O'Kellys and de Soleilles married each other, Patrick Boland's sister Gertie married the bride's brother Patrick O'Byrne de St Gery. My mother told me she could never understand how my father had managed, in the general stampede, not to marry one of the two remaining O'Byrne de St Gery girls—they never did marry anyone else.

Many years later when, at the age of twenty-one and still imbued with the romance of that background of the *grande réunion*, I wrote my own first novel called *The Wild Geese*, I had a letter from Gerald O'Kelly de Gallagh in Paris. He had come across on a Paris bookstall a catechism compiled in French, Irish and English for the instruction of the mixed-language men of the Brigade by one of its chaplains, dedicated on the flyleaf by the author to an ancestor of his own, General O'Kelly of Louis XIV's army. He asked if I would like it, but alas the War broke out and such compliments were forgotten. This Gerald O'Kelly was a wit; accused after the War of being a collaborator because he had sold his champagne to the occupying Germans, he asked his accusers if they had ever drunk that particular cru themselves. It was advertised by a picture of a man drinking a glass of water with a disgusted expression and exclaiming 'Oh, quel eau!', while an equally disgusted girl drank a glass of milk, crying 'Oh, quel lait!'; and finally they were shown toasting each other with champagne, exclaiming delightedly 'O'Kelly!' 'I could hardly have sold that stuff to Frenchmen,' he said, 'and it must have kept hundreds of Germans out of the front line for months.'

After the *grande réunion* my father and my uncle were called to the bar in London, my father living in the Temple, but the cause of Irish nationalism had been gradually gripping them both, and shortly after, both still in their early twenties, they decided to stand for Parliament. My father got in for South Kerry, but my uncle Patrick failed, decided he was not cut out for public life and was bored by the Law, and taking a house in Galway retired to his library and remained there, practically without moving from it, for sixty years. He read voraciously on every conceivable subject, books overflowed the shelves till, with his copious notes, they were stacked high on every flat surface in the room including the floor. He talked brilliantly, corresponded with scholars in many languages and never published a line.

Can there be a gentle fanatic? Can a single-minded yet not be a one-track-minded man? How can I describe my father or his influence in a house where my mother's could not but be the dominant personality?

In the first place, he was beautiful. I once asked the family friend Gerald Fitzmaurice why when practically every other member of the Irish Parliamentary Party had at one time or another been sent to gaol my father, while expressing all the same opinions and making the same proscribed demands, never had. He smiled. 'How could anyone arrest a man with a face like that?' Well over six foot tall, with an athlete's figure all his days, with eyes of a very light but startling blue, he exuded a kind of intelligent innocence which is a rare combination. As youngsters we were always afraid of shocking him, not for our own sakes but for his. My mother or one or other of us would often read aloud while the others sewed or mended and my father liked to listen, and, someone once suggesting a book we considered amusing if rather coarse, my youngest sister said: 'Do you think Daddy's quite old enough?' He had a bloom that you would hate to rub off.

Our friends had the same feeling. One, daughter of a school friend of his, who was staying with us during the War, had been out on the tiles one night with some Free Frenchman, Free Pole, or Free Norwegian, and was just about to slip into the house at seven in the morning with the intention of appearing at breakfast as though straight from her respectable bed when my father came out, on his way, as usual to the seven o'clock Mass. 'Hullo, dear,' he said. 'Been to the early?' This meant, of course, the six o'clock Mass, the only, to him, conceivable reason for a girl coming home at such an hour. Some twenty-five years later she told me she was still haunted by the guilt of having lied to him, but I reassured her: if she had told him the truth he would only have thought how kind it was of her to bestow her charming innocent young company on some lonely allied soldier so far from home.

Politically he had a constitutional inability to hate his opponents which must have been a handicap, and 'misguided' or 'misled' seemed to me the strongest condemnation of which he was capable. But if I am to explain his politics, and the influence they had on our childhood (and, indeed, on our whole lives), I must beg the gentle reader's indulgence for a moment while I broach, as briefly as possible, The Irish Question, while guaranteeing on my honour not to attempt to answer it.

In a nutshell, the question was 'Who should govern that particular section of the group known for some time geographically as the British Isles?' It was a question that came nearer to finding an answer in my father's youth than at any time before since the

11th century, and a great deal nearer than it has since.

It was the cultural aspect (oddly, to us now) that first appealed to my father. There had been no truly indigenous Irish culture since its flowering in the 7th century and its death, with the coming of the Anglo-Normans, in the 11th. In Dublin in the 'nineties there was a re-discovery of the Irish language, a throwing off of the culture that had produced Goldsmith, Swift and Sterne and was still producing Wilde and Shaw. Everyone in Dublin was writing, either in the hybrid style of Yeats and Synge (using Irish-language inspiration, and even its constructions, in English) or in the Irish-dialect-English of O'Casey and Joyce. The specifically Irish theatre was being born, with Lord Dunsany and Lady Gregory at the *accouchement*, and the talk of the clubs and drawing-rooms was spreading thence to the pubs and street corners, whose habitués began writing too. It was a heady atmosphere.

From that world one face I never saw remains with me: the face of Maud Gonne. A lifetime after those Dublin days when her beauty reigned supreme, my father was in bed with a cold when I brought the morning paper with his breakfast and said as I gave it to him: 'It says here Maud Gonne died.' He was in his eighties then, but as he heard me his face changed as I should never have believed a face could: the lines of age were smoothed clean away, the eyes, a little misted, shone a clear and startling blue, and a young man was staring up at me. 'Maud Gonne,' he said, 'she couldn't!' And then the years flowed back. 'Ah, well,' he said, 'I suppose, come to think of it, she must have been getting on.' He had never approved of her politics which were far too extreme for him; but another aspect of her hold on the period struck me that same night. I had been down to Brighton to see the opening of a new play, and was coming back on the last train, alone in a carriage with a very drunken old Irish workman, who was singing rebelly songs as he lay full length along the seat opposite me. We had an hour's journey ahead of us, so—'Been celebrating something good?' I asked, in my best Kerry accent.

He squinted across at me. 'You wouldn't understand at your age.' he said. 'Maud Gonne died, and it was to her I was drinking.'

'She was a friend of my father's,' I said, fascinated, 'did you know her?'

'I did,' said he. He had been on the run after the 1916 Rising, and she had given him shelter. 'She washed my socks, and she gave me a second pair. And says she to me "Do you keep those washed, now, every night one pair or t'other. A man on the run needs look after his feet." And I did, and here I am to tell you: Maud Gonne died to-day.'

Well, to get back to the Irish language: my father, with his passion for Greek, might well have been content with the ancient texts which he bought eagerly as they were published; but to my Uncle Patrick living languages had more appeal. Bicycles had recently come into their lives, and they set off on a cycling tour of the South and West where little English was yet spoken.

My father discovered to his horror that practically no-one could read and write. In such schools as there were, only English was allowed to be taught, and, particularly in mountain country where they might be six or eight miles from a school and with no transport of course, if the children attended at all the lessons were in a language they didn't speak, and the teachers were even forbidden to answer questions in Irish. Naturally enough, the language movement rapidly became inextricably entangled with Nationalist politics. Higher Education had until 1829 been an entirely English prerogative in Ireland, the natives being debarred from University (Trinity College, Dublin), the learned professions, and commissioned rank in the services by their religion. Those who could afford it sent their sons to universities abroad, although this was also illegal; but few could afford it, as (in an entirely agricultural economy) they were not allowed to acquire the title deeds to land or to pass on such land as they had intact to their eldest sons, and holdings became therefore ever smaller and smaller. They sometimes resorted to such devices as having a junior member of a family become nominally Protestant and hold the land for his senior (it was not done for the head of the house to besmirch his honour in this way). Although many of these disabilities had been lifted some sixty years before my father became interested in educational problems, there had not been time in a country devastated in the interval by the famine years for the natives to build up the capital to endow universities for their children to attend (Trinity being still exclusivist), and the government saw no need. The permitting of the teaching of Irish in schools and the setting up of the National University became for many years my father's chief political interest.

It may be necessary here to explain that the terms Catholic and Protestant in Ireland have minimal doctrinal significance, and the policies described above were only for a short time, if at all, primarily religious persecution. Henry VIII, for instance, from whose time some of them date, always considered himself, doctrinally speaking, still the Defender of the Faith that a Pope had dubbed him. But the Irish were an unruly lot. The Normans, everywhere they went, including England, had the gift of merging very quickly into the landscape; but the English had not. When Elizabethan nobles sent to rule Ireland adopted the expedient of enclosing 'within the Pale' the centre of the country and excluding from it anyone who was not prepared to let them live in peace, it was no use asking a man if he was Irish or there would have been no-one to work the expropriated land: you asked him if he was Protestant, and if he said he was, you could be sure that he had accepted the new order; if he said he was not, you sent him outside the Pale or put him under restrictions that would make it impossible for him to gain power within it. Beyond the Pale were outlaws, where the rule of law did not run, and if you had to go there you took your life in your hands (particularly on the borders of the Pale) where the men you had dispossessed scratched a living, and you acted accordingly. The natives looked to France and Spain, which they regarded as still part of Christendom, for help; and France and Spain were your enemies, so that anyone who did not accept your new order was demonstrably your enemy too. There is no word in the Irish language (which alone, outside the Pale, was spoken at that time) for Protestant except the word for Englishman: Sassenach. Anyone who went over to the Sassenach was regarded as what the 20th century would call a collaborator, and still is. Came more landless English soldiers with Cromwell, their disciplined ranks quite unable to deal with the guerilla warfare they found themselves subjected to; and it was a useful bonus to the government to have such expropriated land as fell vacant, when those who still refused to accept the new order were sent 'to hell or Connaught', with which to reward their loyal men. By that time Catholic meant Irish as much as Protestant meant English; and although, after two or three hundred years, some of the newly-landed English gentry might think of themselves as Irish by right if not of purchase at least of tenure, the natives never did; and the division of the inhabitants into 'Catholics' and 'Protestants' made it easier, semantically, to distinguish between right-minded and wrong-headed citizens. It really had very little to do with the Thirty-nine Articles. It still has.

So largely from a desire to secure better education, particularly in the South and West, my father became actively Nationalist. The family always had been so inclined. During the rising of 1798, the land they then farmed near the Curragh in Kildare had been attacked by troops, and their barns, mills and house destroyed, and they had migrated to Dublin. Mills of any size were then rare in Ireland, for the Irish staple diet was potatoes, not bread, and the English gentry milled usually on their own estates enough for their own domestic needs. There was a demand for bread in Dublin, however, and the Bolands set up large mills to supply it. During the potato famine in the 1840's they owned practically the only ones able to afford the equipment to mill the maize the government allowed to be imported to feed the population, and the family fortunes were established—not, I hope (but have sometimes suspected), on too heavily profiteering a scale. My grandfather's farming, now at Raheny Park in northern County Dublin, cannot have brought in much for the till, for it was highly experimental. He passionately disapproved of farmyard manure, for instance, incredible loads of it having been stored rather than sold lest anyone else should use it and thereby destroy their land, while he believed equally passionately in the beneficial effects of clover on the soil, to the point of growing practically nothing else. Politically he was keenly involved in the Agrarian Reform movement and was one of the founders of the Tenants' Defence League and provided its headquarters in Dublin. When he died the farms were sold and the mills were turned into a public company—but got into the history books by being used as a sort of fortress headquarters in 1916 by De Valera, and the Sinn Feiners of whose violence my father so deeply disapproved.

The object of the Nationalist Parliamentary Party which he joined in the late 'nineties was to obtain by parliamentary means what we should now call devolution—self-government for Ireland under the Crown. There had been a parliament in Dublin for a short time in the 18th century, but since no Catholic was eligible it was not considered by the Irish to represent them. From 1829 it became possible for Catholics to be elected to Westminster, and from then on the campaign for self-government grew, though bill after bill was defeated. Considering that Ireland's economic and strategic interests must always bind her to Great Britain, no such thing as an independent republic, or even control over their own foreign affairs, was envisaged by the Party; and it seems odd now that such passions were aroused against their rather modest demands. For over half a century the country voted over-whelmingly for these demands, and the remarkable thing is that its confidence in the Party was such that for all that time its policy of non-violence was supported. It must be remembered that there was no payment of Members in those days, and they were therefore respected as demonstrably dedicated men. Only about half a dozen of the sixty-odd Members were at all rich; having to be in England during the session and in Ireland during the recess, no trade or profession such as was possible to English Members could be carried on by them (my father, for instance, could not practise at either the Irish or the English Bar); most were farmers, whose land had to be managed by their families as best they could in their absence. Party funds there were, but they were raised from subscriptions of a few pence a week from supporters, mostly farm labourers and smallholders paying exorbitant rents. Parliamentary ambition of the ordinary kind there could be none, for Members were required by the Party to take an oath never to hold office in any Government until Home Rule was granted. Members who had somehow to pay for rooms and their keep in London in such a situation had to be dedicated indeed.

Violence being tabu, the only weapon the Party had was the parliamentary system itself, and it flung itself gleefully into the ruthless manipulation of it: if Ireland was not allowed to govern itself, then England shouldn't be allowed to either. The device in which my father particularly delighted was the turning of every debate on any subject whatever into a discussion of Irish problems. You had to remain technically in order, of course. The finest example of this technique was felt to have been reached by the brilliant wit Tim Healey, when he turned a whole debate on some contribution or other of England to the Polish State Railways into an exposé of the terrible state of transport in Ireland, without the Speaker being once able to rule him out of order. My father became known as 'the Member for Malta'—his concern for Irish education leading him to use this technique in debates on Imperial affairs, using the suppression of the Maltese language and the consequent state of education there as his nominal parallel. Having had a lot of fun with this, however, being my father, he became seriously involved with the problems of the Maltese themselves, eventually achieving the recognition of Maltese in the Courts as well as the schools there.

Soon his knowledge of the subtler points of parliamentary procedure became encyclopaedic. 'The poor dears,' he told my mother, 'don't know their own silly business.' This, and his charm and popularity with his fellow Members, and the fact that his English education enabled him to get on well with other parties as well, made him very early on a natural choice as a Whip. And then the fun really began.

The manipulation of pairing was a particularly fine art; when he didn't want one of his own flock to provide a pair for a Member who didn't want to attend, he would most obligingly arrange for a pair from another party to be available—always a man who he happened to know had some private quirk of conscience or policy, which would in the final resort have caused him to vote, had he been present, the same way as the man he was pairing with, against Irish interests. Snap divisions were another of his fortes. We lived only a few hundred yards from the House, and another Irish Member lived even closer. They would each invite hordes of the Party to a buffet dinner on the same night: a single Member would be left holding the fort and he, when the government Whips had let their own Members drift away, would nip out of the chamber and telephone; and the guests would pelt along the Embankment, force a division, and carry the vote. Soon it became unsafe for the unfortunate English ever to go home at all. 'If they want their dinners or their sleep, poor dears, let them give us Home Rule,' he said.

On one occasion more elaborate measures were taken. In mid-session, an important mass meeting in Ireland was suddenly called on an issue of burning importance, and was heavily advertised. Knowing that some Members would have to attend it, the Government promptly arranged an important debate in the House. With noisy expressions of regret and indignation, the Party almost en masse took the night mail from Euston the night before, left the train at the only stop before Holyhead, crossed the line, steamed back to London, and descended on the House. One of my earliest recollections of my father is of his appearing at breakfast after an all-night sitting with no voice. 'Cheering,' he whispered. 'We defeated the Government.' That may well have been the occasion.

There were many wits in the Party, and debates must often have been highly amusing. On one occasion a humourless Orange Member from Ulster called Thomas Massey was complaining about the use of the suffix 'Mass' in such official words as the names of Law Terms—'Christmas' and 'Lammas' should be changed to 'Christ-tide' and 'Lammas-tide', he said. 'Admirable,' said Tim Healey, surprisingly supporting the motion, 'and the Honourable Member for South Down will of course be known as Mr Totide Tidey.'

After the creation of the Republic, a Mr Boland was once appointed Irish Ambassador to London. Searching for someone he might know in England with whose presence to compliment him at a dinner on his appointment, the Foreign Office invited my father, presuming him a relation, and put him next to the Ambassador. Making conversation to this total stranger, my father remarked that the humour seemed to have gone out of politics in London since the departure of the Irish Members— how was it in the Daìl? The Ambassador looked shocked. Did my father really think politics was the place for humour, he asked. When later as Ambassador to the United Nations he was taking the chair, on an important occasion he lost control of the debate and smashed the gavel in his attempt to command silence. 'Poor dear,' said my father, 'it wouldn't occur to him to get them laughing.'

He loved debate, and encouraged all of us to enjoy the art of argument. If you were losing, he would think of a good point on your side and, turning his head to your angle and putting on a high squeaky voice, he would make it on your behalf, and then whisper, 'Go on from there, dear.' He was, my mother told me, a clever and cogent speaker, sure of his facts, rather than an orator, better in the House than on a platform. He hated anything approaching rabble-rousing. 'Before you know where you are, you'll have a rabble roused,' he would say, 'and for too long that's been too easy to do, in Ireland.' Throughout his parliamentary career he was only once opposed in South Kerry—it wasn't worth anyone's while to try.

In 1912 the Home Rule Bill was passed through the Commons at last, then by the Lords, and it received the Royal Assent. It was going to take some time to put it into operation, of course— and meanwhile Sir Edward Carson raised and trained the Ulster Volunteers, armed from Germany, to fight the British Army (there wasn't an Irish one) to prevent this happening. There was a pause in the implementation of the Act, those in high places knowing that war with Germany was imminent, and the deflection of troops to suppress the Orangemen presented a problem. Germany, believing that England would be otherwise engaged, invaded Belgium. The Prime Minister consulted the Irish Party: would they agree to the postponement of implementation of the Act till the War should be over? The following day, he announced England's support of Belgium in the House, and John Redmond, leader of the Irish Party, rose. Carson had said of his Volunteers, 'Ulster will fight and Ulster will be right.' Redmond announced the Party's agreement to the suspension of the Home Rule Act, ending, 'Ireland will fight beside you—and Ireland will be right.'

But alas there were those who thought the Party had betrayed their country. 'England's danger is Ireland's opportunity,' quoted the extremists, and by 1916 they had enough support to stage the Easter Rising. It failed, except as a diversion, but it, and the brutality with which it was suppressed by the only (irregular) troops available, who became known as the Black-and-Tans, spelled tragedy for relations between the countries.

In Ireland, of course, there had to be humour in the tragedy. During the Rising, it is told, the lookout for a group ambushing the Black-and-Tans saw a man approaching along the dark country road. 'Halt! Who goes there?' said he. 'Jesus, Mary and Joseph!' exclaimed the startled farm labourer. 'Pass, the Holy Family,' said the lookout, 'and all's well.' During the subsequent troubles, one angle of Merrion Square was so often involved in such incidents that it was know as Ambush Corner. My Aunt Mary, a maiden lady well known for her prison visiting and other good works, came to this corner early one morning, and hesitated when she saw men there engaged in a machine-gun duel with some others some way off on her own doorstep. One of the men on the corner held up his hand, and shouted to the enemy: 'Hold on a moment, boys—here's Miss Boland coming home from Mass!' The shooting stopped, Aunt Mary tripped across the Square and up the steps, bowing and smiling her thanks to the contestants, and closed her door—and the battle continued.

After education, my father's chief political interest was in Irish trade. The Irish were chronically poor. As for everything else in Ireland, there were of course historical reasons for this: the 'penal laws' had made a nation of agricultural labourers, paid largely in kind, and tenant farmers on tiny holdings on the estates, all too often, of absentee landlords whose agents' livings depended on 'rack-renting'. My mother once visiting a cottage where the field visible from the road before the house was a stony waste on which struggled a miserable crop, was amazed to see from the back windows a superb vegetable garden and fields beyond where everything flourished as it can in the Gulf-Stream climate and rich soil of Kerry if you can only clear the stones and boulders in the pockets of the hills. The cottager laughed and explained that my mother would always find it so: any land that the agent could see from his horse as he rode by was 'land you could do nothing with', or he would put up the rent; but he was too lazy to leave the road, and if you were lucky enough to have fields out of his sight you could live off them yourself. As late as the famine of 1847–9 Ireland's was not a money economy at all, and the British Government simply could not understand why the people could not (they presumed would not) buy the maize they sent over for them to eat at a few pence a bushel: pence they did not have, their work being rewarded with the patch on which they could grow potatoes. In the fifty or so years since then conditions had improved, but not much; and though land-yields per acre were high particularly in the midlands, the money was all too often still spent in England by those who came over for a few months a year at most for the hunting and shooting.

There still was to all intents and purposes no middle class to keep money moving: there were the gentry and the people. This was because there was no industry to speak of. In ancient times linen had been grown all over Ireland, and the trade had boomed—

but this was at the expense of the growing English woollen industry. The Tudors introduced sumptuary laws that forbade the wearing of linen except by the nobility; anybody else might even be buried only in a woollen shroud. James I, keeping his Scottish subjects sweet by granting expropriated land to any landless men who would accept it just over-the-way in the new Plantation of Ulster, made trading facilities which promoted the linen industry there, but it had died out in the South and was never re-introduced on any scale.

Industry there must be, my father felt, and he tried everything. It must be admitted that in his own efforts to establish it he was spectacularly unsuccessful. On his youthful travels he had been impressed by New Zealand flax. Now, there must be a use for that , and in the nearly sub-tropical climate of Kerry, at any rate, it would surely flourish. He tried it out, and flourish it did. When I went back when I was eighteen to Derrynane, where we had lived when I was a child, you couldn't get up the drive for the way tall jungle growths of it had closed in on either side. But nothing ever came of it. When he first married, he and my mother used to go on fishing trips to Norway (where they met Arnold Lunn, and my mother, who knew Switzerland so well, advised him where best to try his surprising plan to introduce the Norwegian practice of ski-ing there), and my father had been impressed by the timber industry. Ireland had been denuded of forests, but the mountains of Kerry were no more rugged than those of Norway—might he not start a timber industry there? He did. The goats ate the tops off his new plantations, and on those bald eroded hills there was not depth of soil enough anyway. Lace-making—there was already Irish lace made in Limerick, and it was a thing that particularly lent itself to cottage industry, the very thing for the scattered cabins in the Kerry hills. He brought instructors to Kerry, and collected boxes and chests and crates of Irish lace of every kind he could find, and arranged for an exhibition of it in London to drum up orders. But lace was out of fashion, and we ended up with enough to dress a nation in our own London attics. My mother edged everything she could think of with it, and we certainly had very wonderful tablecloths, but cottage industry there was none.

Something he could do, however, for the Ulster linen industry and for the Irish bacon trade. Much Danish bacon and foreign linen was being sold in England as Irish. My father patented an Irish trade mark and steered through parliament a 'national trade marks act' which would make such practices illegal. 'You'll be asking us to stamp "Made in Ireland" on the eggs to go with the bacon next,' laughed Members of Parliament. 'Why not,' said my father, who had no idea if you could, 'and the date as well to show how fresh they are.' It is interesting to think that this was the first national trade mark, and the origin of later protective practices of insisting on imports being marked 'Made in Japan' and so on. Meanwhile he was pressing for land reform, and for improvements to Irish Railways that alone could make the establishment of industry and development of trade on any scale a practical proposition. One last effort he made at helping things along himself: during the war he financed a scheme called The Irish Direct Supply Association, which was to be a co-operative of farmers trading direct to the hungry English markets without the use of profiteering middlemen. He got in a highly recommended expert to handle the business end—who promptly departed (to Spain, it was thought) with the funds.

There was no Interpol in those days and my father (waiting till the next recess, of course) went to Spain to pursue his own researches.

'And did you find him?' I asked eagerly. My father was smiling reminiscently.

'Find who, dear?'

'The man who stole all your money!'

'Oh, him, poor man, no—but, you know, they're absolutely right: one's first sight of the Alhambra *must* be by moonlight.'

The effects of the Easter Rising, and the bitterness between the two countries it engendered, spelt the ruin of my father's life's work, the destruction of his conviction that parliamentary means without resort to violence would eventually bring justice and peace. He remained on in Parliament while the Party survived; but when England finally gave way to the threat of renewed civil war, and agreed to the lunacy of partition with its inevitable future of eternal strife, his heart was broken. My mother never went back to Ireland. For years my father couldn't bring himself to go back either, but bitterness was not in his nature, and by the 'thirties he was going back every summer, staying with his brother Patrick, and touring round the rest of the family, but never visiting Kerry again.

Then in 1940 my eldest sister Honor told Maureen and me that Fred Crowley had asked her to marry him. What on earth would this do to my father? Fred at the age of sixteen had run away from home to join the I.R.A. in the Easter Rising, and had now for years been a member in the Dàil, for part of my father's old constituency in South Kerry. We decided to introduce him initially just as a friend. We sat on the edges of our chairs to watch how they would get on. Fred was paralysed at first, but after a while mentioned a part of the constituency where he was trying to get a road built. My father, who had been politely struggling to keep some sort of conversation going with this poor dear shy young man, sat up, 'Do you mean to tell me they haven't built that road yet?'

'They have not! Would you believe it!'

'And the bridge to Valencia Island?'

'Nor that!'

They were off, roads and bridges and schools and local industries—it was the well-being of the Kerryman that was really all either of them cared about. So Fred and Honor married— and that was a great wedding. It was wartime, and Fred, as an ex-member of the I.R.A., was followed everywhere while in England by Special Branch men. At the wedding reception he recognised from a window two of them hanging 'unobstrusively' about the Square outside. He asked my brother, on leave from the R.A.F., if 'it isn't a shame for them, poor dears?' Poor dears! He was the right son-in-law for my father all right! He and Brendan went down and asked the poor dears in, as a more comfortable way to keep an eye on him; and so they joined the party, and my father had a fascinating conversation with them about their work. There-after he often stayed with Honor and Fred in Kerry, where everyone welcomed him. When Fred died Honor took on the constituency and sat for it for twenty-five years, so that it was a 'rotten borough' in the family for nearly seventy. And when she died the whole town of Killarney went into mourning with flags at half mast on all the public buildings, and the President and the entire Cabinet and most of the Opposition front bench came down to join the 'mountainy men' who came from all over Kerry for the funeral. Several of the latter said to me: 'Yours is a wonderful family, Miss Boland, you'd never know any of them were politicians at all.'

An English tourist in the French village where we spent our summers once said to me: 'What a beautiful voice your father has! I'd love to sit under him.' The expression, which I had not heard before, startled me until I learned that it meant she would like to hear him preach, his appearance and manner having evidently persuaded her he must be some kind of a parson. He never lost his Irish accent. We used to love to make him tell the story of how he 'had had one' when he and Uncle Patrick first went to school in England and were asked if they could play cricket. He replied: 'We can. (No true Irishman ever said 'Yes' or 'No', but—a legacy from the Gaelic language—'I can' or 'I can't'.)—Oim dthe bathrr and me brother's dthe bowlrr.' We could hear very little difference from his normal speech. One of his contemporaries at school was Hilaire Belloc, who had a slight French 'r', and they were mercilessly teased for their accents, particularly in the Latin plays which they performed every year, in which, they were told, they sounded even funnier than in English. I still have a Plautus and three Terence texts (heavily Bowdlerised, I suspect, 'ad usum puerorum') marked with their headmaster Cardinal Newman's production notes and several vowels and consonants underlined by my father in an effort, I am sure, to eliminate this cause for mirth. Luckily he never succeeded.

None of us ever caught his accent, and I was quite unaware that I had evidently caught something of his style of speech until a very distinguished actor once wanted to throw up a part in a play of mine: he had never before in his life, he said, finished the second week of rehearsals without having being able to learn his lines. 'Oh, if that's all,' said another of the cast, 'neither can I: she's un-learnable.' Appalled, I asked other actors who had been in plays of mine if they had found the same trouble. They all agreed that my lines were hell to learn, the words were all in a just very slightly unexpected order. 'Like Shaw,' said several (and my father's accent was very like Shaw's). I suddenly realised that I had caught an Irish twist to a phrase which had got into what was meant to be English dialogue. Thus, I suppose, are the sins of the fathers visited upon the children. Ah, well, there is nothing you can't get absolution for if you have 'a firm purpose of amendment'.

Forty

---∘◦◉◦∘---

Until 1918, when I was five, we lived in Ireland when Parliament
was not sitting. Having no house of his own in his constituency of
South Kerry, my father rented Derrynane from the O'Connels, a
rambling 18th- and early 19th-century house by the ruins of a
Cistercian abbey, on the wild, rocky coast at the south-western-
most tip of the country, 'the next parish to America'. The Cister-
cians seem to have had an unerring eye for a romantic landscape,
for Derrynane was more beautiful even than their other abbey in
Kerry, at Muckross on the Lakes near Killarney. In our day the
Gulf Stream, now moving away, so warmed the coastal waters
that you could bathe all the year round, and the rock-pools were
bright with sea-anemones. We lived barefoot and ran wild, seals
basked on the foreshore, everyone caught enormous fish, and the
bats were chased out of the bedrooms every night with tennis
racquets, which I thought was the meaning of the words 'to bat',
so that a ball, in my mind's eye, always had invisible wings. We
were twenty miles from anywhere, and also from a doctor, and my
mother luckily timed five pregnancies so well as to ensure that
we were each born during a session, and so in London. 'Never
mind,' said my father, 'you were all conceived in Daniel O'Connel
the Liberator's bed.' Those early years made an indelible impression on something in me, but more I think on my sense of
romance than on my memory. I would have said that I re-

membered Derrynane as vividly as anything in my life; but when I went back there for the first time when I was eighteen I have to admit that I discovered my whole vision of it was pure imagination. The feel was right, the detail was right, but the geography in what I had thought was my memory was evidently entirely my own invention. Perhaps a child absorbs atmosphere and the discoveries of its own vivid, near-to experience, but not spatial relationships, and I had put my rock-pools full of tendril-waving anemones into the landscape of a dream. I took off my shoes and stockings, and the rough-smooth mountains felt crisply right to the soles of my feet, but the skyline was all in the wrong order. It may be that this is what an artist does with his childhood experience of the world.

We commuted between this earthly paradise and, during parliamentary sessions, 40 St George's Square, our house in Pimlico just along the Embankment from Westminster Abbey. It was always known as Forty, and always seemed to all of us the perfect house-shaped house, which all others presumably tried but failed to imitate. Pimlico was a village, bounded on the north by the Buckingham Palace Road and on the south by the River. When the wind was easterly we heard the chimes of Big Ben, and when it was westerly the bugle calls of Chelsea Barracks. It had one little street of shops—a butcher, a baker, a laundry, and a newsagent where you could buy the children's papers *Puck* and *Rainbow*, and also sweets, rarely allowed. The whole area had been marshland until some fifty years before, and an ancient botanist friend of ours called Mr Britten had, as a small boy, picked rare marsh flowers on the site of our house. It was re-claimed when it came into the Duke of Westminster's family, and town-planned as no part of London then was, designed and built by Cubitt. Eccleston and Warwick Squares at the northern end of the area called it South Belgravia, but we true natives knew it was

Pimlico, and in the family, with our sense of divided national backgrounds, we called ourselves Pimlicuddlians.

Our house, like those in all three squares linked by the Belgrave Road, was five stories high with a basement; painted white, with two pillars supporting a portico and balcony onto which the drawing-room windows opened. All the back streets had smaller houses of exactly the same design except for the lack of one storey. It was (and I will hear no argument to the contrary) very beautiful. The Square gardens (which were, as it happens, oblong) were well designed and planted, and kept up in our time by two gardeners each. At the end of ours was the church of St Saviour's, Pimlico, whose neo-gothic spire, decorated with niches which were never intended to hold anything so papistical as statues of saints, seemed to us quite beautiful too, to me even in my twenties when I stood on the doorstep admiring it in the light of the fires of the London Blitz. By that time all the other houses in the Square were subdivided into flats, and the back streets had become, frankly, a near slum; but we loved it better than I could do now, when the little houses have become smart and have doors painted in improbable colours with 'antique' carriage lamps on each side of them.

I cannot imagine why, when the rest of the road round the Square had been given a perfectly ordinary modern surface, a strip a yard and a half wide leading from Forty to the gate in the iron fence round the garden had been left still paved with cobble-stones. There were three other gates on each side of the Square and one at the River end, and none of them were approached by cobbled strips. As children we considered ours a suitable honour paid to Forty and to *the* gate. Grown-ups felt differently about it, for the wooden wheels of the many vehicles that still had them made a terrible clatter going over it. The Army and Navy Stores delivery van, for instance, was horse-drawn even into the 'thirties, and 'Stores' horse, Stores' horse,' Anne would cry, and rush down for two lumps of sugar. When my mother was expecting a baby thick straw would be laid across the strip even as late as 1916 when Eily was born, but thereafter I suppose there were not enough wooden wheels left to distrub people's rest. One summer while we were in France our sacred cobblestones were removed, and we were most indignant that we had not been consulted; but how much noisier London must have been before tarmac was invented than with the traffic that shatters delicate modern nerves.

To me no trees have ever seemed more beautiful than the planes in the Square. Not like your forest trees with clumsy great branches springing from near the ground and wriggling along like the trunks of elephants searching for buns, ours grew sheer for twenty feet or more and then wept down in romantic curtains, their leaves a dusty yellowish grey-green like the soft colours in a faded tapestry; and the tallest of all hung, of course, over *our* gate. It was the favourite, too, of the starlings that flocked into it in hordes at dusk. In the autumn we would watch fascinated the small false starts that a few would make time and again to migrate, until suddenly at some secret signal which we were always sure we should one day identify, the whole cloud of them would rise at once and be gone till the next year. Then would come the 'bobbles' that we loved on the trees—how do you mean, 'nasty, sooty things'?—and Fred would have to come and remove bucketfuls of seeds from the gutters. Then we would wait for the forsythias, the lilacs, the mock-oranges, and lean on the railings of the flowerbeds (which you must not climb over to retrieve lost balls, however new and precious), to watch the gardeners digging up withered tulips and planting geraniums, calceolarias, begonias, and edgings of marigolds, as they did year after year—and how do you mean, 'crude, monotonous, uninspired'? They were what was

(56)

meant by 'All things bright and beautiful', and who could want them changed?

The gardeners were the Old Gardener and St Joseph—the latter so-called because he was exactly like a figure in our Christmas crib. Also, he was a sweet-tempered man who did not dislike all children on principle, as his crotchety colleague did. He could even be persuaded, if neither the latter nor our nurse was looking, to let us take off our shoes and socks and dance in the carefully-aimed spray of his hose on hot days. He would leave little piles of not-so-perfect seedlings on the path and wink at us and look the other way while we stole them for our own back garden; and he would not grub up quite all the weeds out of the grass if we begged him to leave enough for daisy and buttercup chains before the Old Gardener came to check.

There were other children who played in the Square, to which all the inhabitants of the houses round it had keys, notably Mary and Budge Boyd, children of the Vicar of St Saviour's, and Budge's friend Laurence, who really lived in Lupus Street round the corner, but whose father was the Curate, Mr Olivier. The two boys were much older than I, almost Brendan's age, and a cut above playing with us, but kind enough to brave the Old Gardener in search of lost balls. I had a contemporary at school whose name was Vivian Hartley, and I wonder what would have happened if I had ever asked her home in the holidays: she changed the spelling of her first name when she grew up, and became Vivien Leigh. There were some other people with much older children who lived on the other side of the Square called Mr and Mrs Casson, and Mrs Casson was also called Miss Thorndyke because she was an actress, and she thought Laurence was very clever because she had seen him in a school play; but he had apparently been playing a girl's part, which lowered him dreadfully in my esteem.

Of the grown-ups who used to sit in the Square our favourites were the Parrot Ladies. They were infinitely old, and traditionalists in every way: their skirts, even in the 'twenties, swept down to the grass, and their waists, when nobody else had any at all, were pinched in as tight as greyhounds'. There were two of them, and they had two green parrots called, of course, Joey and Polly. The parrots could not fly, and their dialogue was limited to 'Hullo' and 'Dear, oh dear!', but they squawked a great deal. They sat on their owners' shoulders, or walked about on the grass, after which exercise the ladies would pick them up and carefully wipe their feet with lace-edged handkerchiefs. We were allowed to hold them if we sat very still on the grass, but not to put them on our shoulders in case we moved suddenly and they tore our dresses by clinging with their claws; the ladies never moved suddenly, if at all. If they had seen us playing in the Square from their windows before they came out, they would often bring picture books from their own childhood to show us, with little girls in enormous skirts and their knickers hanging down, playing battledore and shuttlecock, and little boys blowing bubbles with churchwarden pipes. They even gave us one, slightly more modern, which I have still. The text which goes with the pictures is in verse of an elevating kind:

> Herbert and Bessie, arm in arm,
> From church are coming home—
> Never from paths of holiness
> May these dear children roam.

The Parrot Ladies disliked our other great friend, Nipper's Mother, for Nipper was a lively fox terrier who chased cats, balls —and parrots. That woman, the ladies considered, should take that dog in the Park. Nipper's Mother, grateful to us for playing ball with Nipper and enabling her to sit fatly on a bench instead of waddling round and round the Square with him, introduced us to the delights of sucking up sherbet from a paper bag through hollow sticks of licorice—a vulgar practice, the Parrot Ladies said, that they were sure our nurse would not approve. So Eily and I always hid the little bags in the elastic-ended legs of our bloomers when nurse appeared with the baby, Anne, in her pram. When Anne was older she made a new friend, 'Mr Capertillar'. She was going through the phase of collecting caterpillars, through which we had all passed, and he told her wonderful things about them and what kind of butterflies they would grow into, bringing her out books with pictures of them which Eily and I enjoyed too. He wrote a humorous piece every day for the *Daily Telegraph*, often quoting Anne, whom he called Felicity Anne because her remarks were so felicitous. Like most humorists he was a sad fellow. He longed to live in the country, and though we thought his writing very unfunny we felt we ought to be kind to him, and invited him to come for walks with us when we were taken to St James's Park to feed the ducks, as they were so countrified. We found he knew all about ducks, and he said that some of these were descended from those established here by Charles II. The keepers knew him, and one of them once took Eily and me across on his tiny punt to the island where the pelicans lived, Anne remaining on the bank clutching Mr Capertillar's hand, convinced that pelicans were carnivorous.

Two other people belonged, in a way, to the Square: Diddle-diddle, who played his barrel organ in the road on Thursday afternoons, and Monday Fiddle. We were not allowed to dance in the street, which our nurse considered unseemly, but might do so just inside the Square gate, by which Diddle-diddle would obligingly park. If we 'danced pretty' under his critical eye we were allowed out one at a time to give three winds of the handle with his hand on it beside ours. Twopence a week pocket-money did not permit of much largesse, but nurse did give him a penny. Monday Fiddle did not play dance-inducing tunes and was regarded as merely an institution, except by Maureen who worried about him because, although he wore mittens in the winter, she felt he was often dreadfully cold. She knitted him an extra thick pair, with double cuffs, and when she grew up and started as a bookseller she always hurried home on Monday evenings to be sure he got his sixpence. He would spot her as she came round the corner from the bus stop, and always play 'Take a pair of sparkling eyes'. He must have been very old, but it was a sad winter when he came no more. The Parrot Ladies and Nipper's Mother had long since gone, even Mr Capertillar had retired to the country at last, and muffins and crumpets grew only in shops instead of under a napkin on a tray, on the head of a man with a bell.

In describing the life in any house one must start with the kitchen. Ours was large, with a monstrous wearisomely black-leaded range which could cook two turkeys at a time, and a vast 'Ideal' boiler which belied its name. It had two windows onto the yard and back garden, beautiful in early summer with two lilacs and a gigantic philadelphus, which kept the kitchen in perpetual twilight for most of the year.

Ruling the kitchen when I was very small was Bridget Cook, so called by then to distinguish her from Bridget Baby (a far less important person).

My mother was no housewife. When she married, she had not been inside a private house for four years; and her entirely hotel-dwelling life had given her no insight at all into how a home was run. She had bought a copy of Mrs Beeton when she got engaged, but, seeing her studying the huge tome, my father said firmly: 'One thing I must insist on, dear: I will *not* have any housekeeping done.' He had a sister-in-law who, of half French and half

Austrian upbringing, was the best housekeeper in Ireland, and still wore a silver filigree chatelaine with all the household keys jingling at her waist. When refrigerators were invented, hers was kept locked up in an old harness-room on the far side of the stable-yard from the house, partly lest it should blow up, but mainly to prevent uncontrolled raids on it. My father suspected that if such methods prevailed he would not be encouraged to bring home half his colleagues in the Irish Parliamentary Party unheralded to dinner. 'Just get a good cook,' he said. My mother closed Mrs Beeton with a sigh of relief and left everything to Bridget Cook.

Running a house, from her point of view, became the art of getting and keeping a good staff, and she had no patience with women who were for ever complaining about servant problems. 'A woman who has servant problems is either stupid, mean or nasty—and probably all three,' she said. Our cook and maids were always Irish, a long way from their own people, and our house had to be made really home to them. They were encouraged to have their friends in (my mother thought the practice of forbidding 'followers' was 'unnatural'), and if they didn't seem to make friends easily she would, through the Parish Priest, find other lonely Irish girls and invite them round. Certainly no servant ever left our house except when they died, or to get married, when they were always given away by my father in morning coat and the same topper he kept for sixty years, and which was known in the family as his 'runcible hat'. When our beloved Kate (who early in my life succeeded Bridget Cook) was dying, in her eighties, the matron at the nursing home said to me: 'Miss Harris is wandering a good deal, I'm afraid. She told me, "I have six beautiful children, foive lovely little gerrls and a boy."' The eldest of us was in her forties then, but Kate's children were us.

However, my mother admired my housekeeping aunt im-mensley, and as each of us grew up we were supposed to learn to do the housekeeping for the year after we left school. In my case this consisted of going down to the kitchen on Monday mornings, and, first of all, 'planning' the meals for the week. I remember well how, on the first Monday, I announced that we would have (my own favourites) roast lamb and treacle tart for lunch that day. 'You will not, Breheda mo van oissle, astoreen,' said Kate—I spell it phonetically as I hear it in my mind's ear; it means 'Bridget, my noble lady, little love'. Kate still slid into Irish, particularly early in the morning, or when annoyed. 'What would I do with all that good cold meat from yesterday?' If I argued she would wish, in Irish/English, 'high hanging on a windy day to you' or 'may the devil make a stepladder of your backbone', and dig her heels in. Very soon my housekeeping degenerated into Kate dictating to me the long weekly order for supplies from the Army & Navy Stores.

Of cooking we learned even less than of housekeeping. I was thirty before I could boil an egg. Excellent cook though she was, feeding a household of ten or twelve was as much cooking as Kate wanted to do, and between whiles she loved to have us in the kitchen as long as she wasn't expected to oversee us 'messing up her clean stove'. She would sing us Irish lullabies and spinning songs, and tell us stories, and teach us slip jigs (she was a beautiful dancer), but let us 'waste good food' she would not. Really I think she did not approve of the notion of our learning to cook on social grounds. Of me in particular she said, 'God shine on you, your mother will have long spinning to make a lady of you anyway.' My mother gave up, but she once said to me, 'Listen to Kate's English, it's pure poetry. She translates literally from Irish half the time,' and she told me that it was in the cottage of Kate's uncle in Kerry, Philly Harris, last of the shannahies (professional story-tellers), that J. M. Synge had bored a hole in the floor of the upper room he rented, to listen to the sort of language he later used in his *Riders to the Sea*. It did not equip me very well for the world of today, but how can you not forgive a woman who sent her daughters to the kitchen to learn poetic diction from the cook?

In the palmy days of Bridget Cook there was also a kitchen-maid, as well as the parlourmaid, housemaid, nurse and nursery maid, and for all of these there had to be a Servants' Hall along the passage from the kitchen, before you came to the pantry; but I remember it best in later years when the staff had shrunk to three and it had become Kate's bedroom, entirely hung with her treasured copies of my father's electioneering posters and photographs of us children in every stage of development. At the end of the passage was the vast icebox (we never did have a refrigerator at Forty), which leaked steadily when the fishmonger remembered to bring the ice, beside the door to the cellar under the road. There was another cellar beside it with a door in the 'area', and both these were knocked together during the Second World War, with those of the houses on either side, to make a continuous shelter and escape route right along the Square. But the Pimli-cuddlians were a defiant lot and only once was it used, when the couple who came were so anxiously plied with cups of tea and extra blankets at intervals all night that they never came again. We ourselves slept, on my father's instructions, in the early days of the Blitz on a row of mattresses along the basement passage, with our 'evacuation suitcases' beside us containing our valuables and some clothes; but one kept removing wanted articles and not replacing them, and on the night when we *were* evacuated because of an unexploded bomb outside, dreadfully worried about what might happen to the house without us to look after it, I personally had nothing in mine but the manuscript of a novel I was working on. All the others' except my father's were even emptier, but they meekly carried them for fear of upsetting him. After that night, feeling that we had had our nearest possible miss, we returned to our own beds for the rest of the War; and Forty suffered no more, except from an oil bomb on the doorstep which merely broke all the windows, ruined the wallpaper in the hall, and was regarded as an insult, it was evidently so cheap and so easily extinguished. When bombs did fall in the vicinity, it was interesting how, on our reclaimed-marsh subsoil, the house could be literally felt, we maintained, merely retreating a step and moving defiantly back into place again. Splendid, valiant Forty!

The garden at the back of the basement suffered from being overshadowed by the whole house at one end, a twenty-foot wall at the other, and nine-foot walls on each side, and was only about twenty-five feet long. It was surprising that the two lilacs and the philadelphus, planted before our time, flowered so well, and not surprising at all that very little else did; but we never gave up hope of creating an earthly paradise. A friend said to me only the other day that she had never seen such tall regale and henryi lilies as she remembered at Forty. Poor dears, they were struggling up to the light, and their height was a good deal more spectacular than their flowers. Gradually we discovered that it was no use breaking our hearts trying to grow the flowers we liked best, and that the books must be believed: only plants with an unnatural passion for dank shade and heavy glutinous clay would flourish. Then we grew day-lilies to perfection, montana and jackmanii clematis up the walls, with winter jasmine and a splendid Mermaid rose. Most of the other plants the books recommended, such as the aconites, were so deadly that we thought of selling off our surplus to would-be poisoners.

All these glories, however, were the product of our later years at Forty. In my childhood the garden was a place to play in rather than to admire. At the far end, three doors in the wall led to cellars under the road, designed to be filled from coal holes in the

(64)

pavement of the back street; but we used the cellars at the front for that purpose. In one, Eily and I proposed to keep Tiny, our dream pony, when we could just devise a lift whereby he could be taken up to the street; and our innumerable designs for this rivalled those, my mother said, of Leonardo de Vinci for aeroplanes. Into one of the others a load of gravel had been poured through the coal hole, and in the other was kept that part of the load which Mr Gatty had sifted for flints, with our eager assistance since we were convinced he was looking for treasure, encouraged in this belief by frequently finding a sixpence he had slipped into the pile we were sifting.

Here I must explain Mr Gatty. He was archivist to the Duke of Westminster, and in this capacity author of many books on the history of London, the best of which was *Mary Davis and the Manor of Edbury*. When the Pimlico marshes were drained, the infill had been brought up-river from, I think, the Wanstead Flats. In the latter area had since been found several flint instruments of its Stone Age inhabitants. A friend of my parents, Mr Gatty had had the gravel brought up from Wanstead to our handy local cellar in the hope of finding others, and thereby proving that under all the Cubitt development of the Westminster estate there was probably archaeological treasure of the kind.

We loved Mr Gatty dearly. Very thin, grey and frail-looking, he must, I think, have dressed like an absent-minded professor, for he wore his superb gold hunter on a bootlace instead of a watch-chain, the Duke having presented it to him on condition that he continued to wear it as he always had his old one. It had a beautiful chime which he would hold to our delighted ears. One day he joined us on our morning walk with our nurse, and changed London for me forever. In Tatchbrook Street on the way towards the Abbey, he explained that the Atch Brook was running under our feet, and, turning through the entrance to Peabody

Buildings, showed us the deep gulley where, in the form of an open storm drain, it could be seen. Thence it disappeared under the Embankment road. It was low tide, and, abandoning our walk to Westminster, he took us across Vauxhall Bridge to show us from the other side where the brook flowed out of a barred watergate into the Thames. That was the first of many walks further afield as we grew older. We followed the Aye Bourne from where Tyburn gallows had stood at Marble Arch to where another tributary joined it under the dip in Bond Street. It had been quite wide here until enclosed in the conduit at Conduit Street, and Mr Gatty took us down into the cellars of Savory and Moore where you could actually hear the water running. When some alterations were being made to these cellars, he had seen Roman stonework with an ancient ring in what had clearly been a dock wall where a ferry boat had once been moored. He showed us, upriver towards Chelsea from our house, where the Wandle, from Wandsworth, entered the Thames as open water just west of Battersea Bridge. Just near it was the little triangular open space outside the King William IV pub which he explained could never be built on, because it had once been a plague pit, consecrated ground where victims had been hastily buried in a common grave.

Apart from the sixpences in the gravel, Mr Gatty never treated us as children, but rather as he might fellow archaeologists being shown over an interesting site he had excavated. The hidden London that he had first revealed to us gave us a different view of all other cities as well, and years later when I lived in Rome I followed the routes of its many 'lost rivers' with just the same feeling.

Back at Forty, on the ground floor was the dining-room with an infinitely extendable table. It was here that my father and the Irish Party's leader, John Redmond, once sat up all night passing between them the pages of Roger Casement's diaries, lent them by Asquith, the Prime Minister, under the blackmailing threat of publishing them in full to discredit the Party if they continued to support the appeal against his being shot for high treason. I have often wondered what my chronically innocent father made of those diaries; it was my mother, not he, who told me the story. It is from this room that my own earliest memory dates: it was Christmas Day, and as the youngest of the family I was given the place next to the official 'stranger for Christmas', an old friend, a barrister accustomed to use his voice rather than his hands at work. I suddenly noticed those hands: they were long, slender and elegant, but the fingertips had no nails and were swollen into terrible great round knobs. I can see them still, and at the time I went into a fit of screaming hysterics and was carried from the room as stiff as a board. My mother explained to me in the nursery that he was not a monster, but a brave, good man, and later I learned that for addressing some banned meeting for Home Rule he had been imprisoned and made to pick oakum, from which he had got an infection, with this lasting result.

As children, however, we normally ate in the nursery dining-room at the far end of the hall, looking over the garden. It was known as Martha's, after the patron saint of women's work, because except at meal times it was the province of a sewing woman who spent three days a week contending with the family's wardrobes and the household linen. Miss Delmont, she was known as Deardelly, because she would make dolls' clothes to match our own. Beside this room was the hand-operated service lift from beside the kitchen below, with a speaking-tube down which you could blow a whistle, and have fascinating conversations with an indignant Kate, from which some of our best Irish swear-words were learned.

Half way along the hall, behind the dining-room, was a bedroom usually occupied by visiting relations. One of these was Aunt Fanny, whose surname, poor woman, was Quirk. A sister of my mother's mother, she was quite mad. To everyone's relief she lived mostly in Rome. She was convinced that she was a saint, and whenever a new one was canonised she took the compliment to herself. The officials at St Peter's were extraordinarily kind to her, for she was a great charmer, and always gave her a seat in a tribune on these occasions. It is the custom in St Peter's, as in the theatre, to clap approval, and Aunt Fanny, correct as always in Vatican dress of black from chin to toes, her head swathed in a black lace mantilla, high above most of the congregation at the front of her tribune, would raise her plump arms in a kind of heavenly benediction over them and acknowledge their applause with gracious smiles and bows. She was well known in Rome for these appearances of hers, and liked for the happy good nature of her harmless mania. But Mussolini came to power, and an Irish-woman, Lady Violet Ashburne, who disliked his policies even in those early days, lobbed a bomb at him. Like so many would-be assassins, her principles were surer than her aim; but the Duce became alarmed: there was another mad Irishwoman loose in the City who had better be removed before she decided like Lady Violet (who had been a friend of hers) that he was the incarnation of evil.

The police at first politely suggested that she returned to her relatives. Alarmed as the pressure increased, Aunt Fanny left her apartment and moved from hotel to hotel; but eventually she was unobtrusively deported. Arrived at Victoria station, she decided to go on to Australia, and moved into the Rubens Hotel 'to wait for a train'. My mother, who at the time knew nothing of the reason for her leaving Rome, sent me, then aged about fifteen and thought to be rather a favourite of her Aunt's, to go through her things and see if I could weed out her more eccentric gar-

(68)

ments on the excuse of lightening her luggage. She clung with particular insistence to 'my Creed', which turned out to be a coat and skirt made by that famous tailor in about 1890, but was otherwise fairly amenable, and invited me to 'take tea' with her in the hotel lounge before leaving. I was of an age to hate to be seen in public with a (still) so oddly dressed relative, and it was late for tea by my standards, but having robbed the poor old dear of half her wardrobe I felt I couldn't refuse. It was over tea that she told me she was being pursued by an Italian gang, led by a man whose name (she whispered) began with M. They had suborned the Italian police, and had followed her from hotel to hotel in Rome. I assured her that the English police were well known to be wonderful, and well able to protect her from Italian gangs, but she suddenly went pale and clutched my arm.

'They're here already,' she gasped, staring wide-eyed at a man sitting across the lounge, 'that man is one of them!'

'But, Aunt Fanny,' I said, 'he couldn't be more English!'

'A disguise,' she whispered. 'I heard him distinctly. He beckoned that Italian-looking waiter and he said "Martini?"— that's the leader of the gang—and the waiter nodded and went away. So he's here too! They followed me to half the hotels in Rome.'

'Oh, Aunt Fanny,' I cried, delighted with my own sophistication, 'he was only asking for a cocktail—that's a modern kind of drink—it's called a Martini. The waiter's gone to get it, you'll see.' She disbelieved me till the waiter duly returned with his drink. Then she laughed at herself delightedly.

'Oh, what a silly old thing I am,' she said. 'And I've been so worried! . . . But you know, dear—don't tell your mother, I don't want to upset her—but I'm being followed by an international gang. The leader is an Italian called Martini. That Englishman over there is one.' So all I had done was promote the Italian gang to international status. I went back to Forty crestfallen, and deposited the problem in my mother's lap.

To continue the description of Forty: half way up the stairs to the drawing-room was a door onto the leads, where there was a roof garden on top of Martha's. Here we used to play a lot, and delight in such excitements in the back street as meetings of the Salvation Army singing, 'Are you washed in the Blood of the Lamb?' to which we would join vociferously if tunelessly in the chorus: 'Yes, I am, *pom*, yes I am!'

In the drawing-room there came to tea every Sunday when we were in London for many years one known to us children, though not, of course to his face, as Fitzie. He was Mr Fitzmaurice to us and to my mother, and to my father Fitzmaurice, though Fitzie (who was a little older) called him John, a subtle distinction in relationships that I relished. As small children we only went into the drawing-room, well washed and brushed, to say 'How do you do?' to visitors, overawed by the huge silver tea tray and its equipment, and dreadfully nervous of knocking over the nasty little occasional tables that held people's cups. Hardly anyone but Fitzie came on a Sunday. He always sat on the same chair, beside my mother's sofa, while my father sat over by the fireplace. Fitzie was short and broad, but wiry, with a hooked nose and a big drooping moustache, and one could see how easily he could pass, as he often had, for a Turk. He always wore brown leather boots that creaked as he sat, forever slowly twirling the foot of one crossed leg. By the time one was about twelve one was promoted, if one liked, to abandoning the heartier nursery tea for the invariable home-made scone and fairy cake of which drawing-room tea consisted, and listening to the most fascinating conversations in the world.

In the days when the Ottoman Empire covered most of the Near and Middle East, there was a British Ambassador only in

Turkey; for the rest of the area there was only the Levant Con-
sular Service, a group of uniquely brilliant specialists. Fitzie alone
divided his time between being for many years permanent First
Secretary at Constantinople and moving as a sort of overseeing
liaison officer about the Levant Service. He was the original of
Sandy Arbuthnot in John Buchan's *Greenmantle*. And his own,
true stories! As a young man, for instance, he had gone, dis-
guised as a Turk, to stay in remote villages, taking a room if
possible overlooking the graveyard, and counting, as they were
buried at night, the victims of a cholera epidemic whose propor-
tions it was suspected that the Sultan's government was con-
cealing. During the Armenian massacres he slipped about the
country amassing the same sort of unreported statistics. In spite
of such things he got on remarkably well with Sultan Abdul-
Hamid, Abdul the Damned; and a series of Ambassadors wisely
left him to do so. He had sat for hours as a young man happily
waiting for audiences in palace anterooms, learning the sign language that the dumb (tongue-mutilated) attendants used between
themselves, from which he discovered more than ever other
Embassies knew from more conventional channels. The sign for
the British Ambassador, I remember, was thumb and first two
fingers rubbed together in a counting-out-money gesture (ah,
those were the days!) while the sign for the Americans was a spit
(and, indeed, a cuspidor was always kept in anterooms for them).
During the First World War he controlled much of Allied Intelli-
gence in those parts—he had been in charge of the Aden Boun-
daries Delimitation negotiations, and knew the desert countries
well, and had had many dealings for years, for instance with Ibn
Saud. He had no time at all for Lawrence of Arabia. 'The fellow
couldn't even speak Arabic,' he said, 'except to give orders.' Of
course, no-one despises an arabist like another arabist, but
Lawrence was a young man finding his way in places where

Fitzie had already spent half a lifetime. 'A tiresome poseur,' he said. 'We sent him to harass a railway line and he wanted to be seen as the gift of Allah to the desert peoples. He promised them all the kingdoms of the world and the glory thereof, and the Middle East is going to be bedevilled by the results for genera-tions.' Fitzie himself was a very early Zionist. 'You can't have a people without a peasantry,' he said, and he saw a homeland in Israel as the true solution of the growing problem of the Jews in central Europe, for which Hitler was soon to find another.

During term-time I used at my boarding school to miss those Sunday afternoon hours, and my mother used to pass on their more romantic contents in letters always beginning: 'Dearest Bridget, as I said to Mark Sykes . . .'—Fitzie's regular prelude. But I was at home when he told us of the fall of Abdul-Hamid. Although he was himself in sympathy with the Young Turks, Fitzie helped the Sultan's family to escape the wrath to come, rescuing the latter's favourite wife from the Summer Palace, galloping away with her in his carriage at night, with a woman servant, both swathed in veils, along the shores of the Bosphorus. 'And I gave the coachman my Colt, and I said to him: "If we're followed, shoot to kill."' A colt, to my mind, was a young horse, and I pictured it on a leading rein galloping along beside the carriage, and wondered why he should so hamper the escape; but one did not interrupt Fitzie in full spate.

When he died, just before the Second World War, my father said to my youngest sister Anne, who was his godchild and to whom he had left some money: 'Whenever you pray for Mummy,' who had died the year before, 'think of Fitzie too.' And I realised that he must always have been aware of what I had come to feel, that poor Fitzie had loved her dearly.

Behind the drawing-room, double doors led into the back drawing-room, its only window darkened by the small conservatory into which it led; and this room was my mother's private province. Here during the years when my father was in the House she coped with all his correspondence, which must have been considerable—certainly when Honor represented the same constituency in the Dáil she received an average of forty letters a day. Here later, when he ran the Catholic Truth Society, she continued to do most of his secretarial work, and edited and wrote herself for the monthly magazine he published. For us, it was the place where stories lived and the best games were played. It was haunted; or rather its doorway onto the drawing-room landing was. All of us, including the servants, going upstairs alone at night used to run past it, particularly if the door was ajar; when you went inside the room there was no sense of haunting at all. We tested it in all sorts of ways, including placing one house thermometer on the door jamb and another on the other side of the landing, but could detect no difference; yet our sometime maid, Maggie, who in her eighties still lives with me, continues to maintain that there was 'a whorrl' in that doorway. My friend Diana Graves, who first came to our house when we were grown up and had never heard the story, writing to thank me for a party, added: 'But you ought to do something about that ghost on your drawing-room landing.'

Above the drawing-rooms were my parents' bedroom and another room always known as the dressing-room but very soon a bedroom for the growing family (as, indeed, both Martha's and the spare bedroom on the ground floor became). Eily and I slept there together for many years. Although there were four years between us, she and I were almost as close as twins. The 'pretend' games we used to play in the daytime were continued, interminable sagas, at night in bed; there was 'Wilds', heavily derivative of the Tarzan and Mowgli stories; 'Finn', based on the heroic Irish legends; 'Tiny', about the mythical pony we owned; and, above all, 'Raoul and Beatrice', continuing after our favourite book, called *My Sword's my Fortune*, ended; it was about the wars of the Fronde; Eily was Raoul and Richelieu and I was Beatrice (I always had to be the girl, for even I had to admit that I didn't look like a boy), and we divided the other characters between us. These 'pretends' were so much a part of my life that years later, when I became a professional writer, I could never get a play or a film script under way until I had had several long sessions with Eily, usually at the Hungarian Csarda restaurant in Dean Street where the backs of the menus were large enough to provide for the taking of copious notes and where, with the aid of much wine, we could construct the story together. Eily became an editor in films, at first as David Lean's assistant and then in her own right, and her technical knowledge was invaluable, but the process was really the same as the night-time storytelling in the dressing-room at Forty, and I've never written anything that was any good since she died.

On the next landing was the only bathroom in the house, with a horrible zinc tank above the bath exactly like that from which the murdered Marat could be seen hanging out, bleeding to death, in the chamber of horrors in Madame Tussaud's. In early days the parents had also hip-baths in their bedroom and dressing-room, as the small children had in the night nursery; but the hauling about by a housemaid of vast copper cans of hot water rightly went out of fashion, and we simply queued up.

On the next floor were three rooms, the day and night nurseries and another bedroom. A little white gate at the top of the stairs prevented us from cascading down to an early death, for we played a great deal on the landing, where stood an immense cupboard of nursery linen and the bulkier of our toys, and a coal bin for the three fires, which had to be replenished by hauling buckets of it up from the cellars seven flights down. The replacing of this system by gas fires was surprisingly long delayed, though the night nursery did have a paraffin heater whose perforated top could be twisted to make an eight-pointed star or a rather terrifying spider shine on the ceiling. We never had nightlights for, like Robert Louis Stevenson, we had 'a lamp before our door', complete with, in my early years, a lamplighter who came to light it with a long pole, 'as he lit so many more', its glowing bowl reflecting up from just below the window, ensuring that none of us was ever afraid of the dark. The two youngest children slept here with Marmie, our nurse, and Wee Wee the nursery maid slept next door.

The day nursery was a sunny room, facing west across roof tops to the River and Battersea and Chelsea bridges. The back of the house was festooned with pipes, far more than the water system could possibly have needed, and my father maintained that if only we knew how to tap them we should find that one contained ass's milk and another champagne. Among these, just outside the nursery window, there nested every year sparrows called Fatherbird and Motherbird; and when one year a nestling fell onto the windowsill and we could not reach the nest to replace it, we put it on cotton wool in a shoe box and fed it brandy to restore it, till it became completely drunk and reeled about on the table, stretching its scrawny neck and squawking, we maintained, for more. It lived, and used often to fly in again when we let it go, perhaps because we continued to put a drop or two of brandy on the bread we left for it on the inner sill till my father complained that the room stank like a bar.

My eldest sister, Honor, was ten when I was born (there were twenty years between the eldest and youngest of us). She was an entirely good little girl, but one always felt that it was because she knew she ought to be, while Maureen, four years older than I, was equally good but because she simply did not know how to be

(75)

anything else. My brother, Brendan, between them in age, was above all an individualist, completely self-contained. He was very gentle, and my mother feared that as a little boy he ought, perhaps, to be what she called 'more fightacious', and gave him soldiers to play with, lining them up in enemy ranks. When she came back into the room they were all arranged in a companionable group on the nursery floor.

'But which is the enemy?' she asked.

'No emily,' said Brendan firmly, 'all friends.' He remained an individualist all his life. After Oxford he went out to Australia, thinking he would like sheep-farming. He got bored working as a 'jackaroo' (trainee) on a station, and joined a gang of nomadic shearers. Gradually he became a complete hobo, often, when he drifted into a town, sleeping under the grandstand of the local race-course, sweeping out a cinema in the morning in exchange for a seat in the afternoon. But he preferred the open spaces.

His serendipity took the form of collecting odd characters in his wanderings, such as one who lived in a shack he had constructed near a creek in the bush, known as Ginger because of his flaming red beard, who conducted a long correspondence with a pen-friend in England, a young girl to whom he signed himself Geraldine and to whom he sent vivid descriptions of his life as the daughter of a rich sheep farmer. Brendan (who called himself Jack in those parts, Brendan being too fancy a name altogether) supplied him with details of such a life as he had seen it from his days as a jackaroo on just such a station, with which Ginger was delighted, and in return showed him a corpse he had recently found in a tree. The man had apparently seen birds flying in and out of a hollow in the trunk and, standing on his saddle (it was just that height from the ground), had felt in the hollow in the hope of finding eggs. The horse had evidently moved away, and the man had lurched with his arm trapped up to the armpit in the narrow hollow. The trunk was large and smooth, there was no branch near, and he had failed, with the fingertips of his one free hand, to get enough purchase to lift his own weight free.

Brendan became known in the district, and the owner of a station, remembering him as an educated man, once sent someone out into the bush where he had recently been seen to ask him if he spoke French and if he could translate what Brendan gathered was some sort of prescription for his wife. Brendan, fearing the woman was ill, jumped on the led-horse the man had brought for him and raced for miles to the station, only to find that it was a French knitting pattern, full of words for such things as purl and plain that he had never heard of. He consoled himself with the thought that he certainly wouldn't have been able to translate much of a medical prescription either.

Eventually, having been sent some books from England that he wanted to settle down and read without humping their load about, he took a job somewhere on the edge of the Central Australian desert tending an artesian well, whose engine had to be filled with petrol every day to pump up water for the sheep. There was a hut for him, with a big store of tinned food, which, with the petrol, was replenished once every two months. Otherwise out of contact with anyone, he happily read, among other things, Paléologue's several-volume history *Le Russie des Tzars*. On one visit of the men with supplies, they found him on the verge of death from starvation, surrounded by food but without the energy to bother to eat it, though he had dutifully serviced the pump engine every day.

After ten years he came back to England, where a friend from his Oxford days gave him a job in the Turkish tobacco trade, studying leaf at the London factory with the object of going to Turkey and eventually setting up a plantation and factory in Rhodesia. My twelve-year-old sister Anne, who had of course never really known him, looked thoughtfully all his first evening at home, six foot five of incredible emaciation, and asked me as we went up to bed: 'Dooka, do you suppose incest is really much fun?' In the war he served in the R.A.F., and then went back into the tobacco trade but soon got bored with it. With his spartanly inexpensive tastes, he had just enough money to live without working, and he could see no reason for acquiring more than he needed. He had three times been engaged to girls— always ones he had met on ships—but had always drifted away short of the altar. He continued to collect odd people, bringing home a fascinating Old China Hand he had met in the docks, a young millionaire meat importer he had got into conversation with about the Argentine at an all-night coffee stall, a busker he had met in a Soho pub when the last of the queues had gone into theatres and cinemas, with wonderful yarns about old music hall days and in need of a bed for the night.

He was what you might call absent-minded about his own clothes. Once, when we lived in Thurloe Square, having run out in the middle of the night of the cigarettes it was no use imploring him not to smoke while he read in bed, he got up and put on a raincoat to go round the corner to the slot machine beside the Rembrandt Hotel. The respectable middle-class patrons coming out from a charity dance were appalled to behold a huge man, stark naked except for bedroom slippers and a transparent plastic mackintosh. A passing policeman, summoned by the doorman to deal with him, asked if he realised he had no pyjamas on. 'Oh, it's all right, thanks,' said Brendan, 'I never wear them,' and only then noticed that he had nothing else very conventional on either.

Once in the same house, which was next to a corner one, Eily and I were giving a party for film and theatre friends, when the corner house was burgled. Friends who knew the owners were away and had seen two men go in and no lights turned on, phoned

the police and watched the door till they arrived to search it. Our
party was much enlivened by the excitement of police cars arriving.
When they had searched the house in vain, the police left one van
outside the door with a handler and police dog in it. Next morning
we asked my brother, who had apparently got bored half way
through the party and drifted off with two of the more congenial
guests to the local pub, who they were. It had been a large party,
and Eily and I didn't know all each other's friends, but it eventually
transpired that Brendan's selected two must have been the burglars,
who had got into our house through an attic window and mingled
with the party: Brendan had indeed noticed that they seemed a bit
out of things, which was why he had chosen them. They talked,
he said, mostly about racehorses, which had interested him.

There had been three large attics at Forty too, above the
nursery floor, originally servants' bedrooms, but as the child
population increased and the servants diminished we took over
one, and another became a sitting-room for Honor and Maureen.
Living up to the standards they had set for behaviour was
difficult for Eily and me, and the nursery landing was a pretty
noisy place, particularly if we were playing 'Wilds'. My taste for
tragic drama developed young, and I was forever dying and taking
an unconscionable time about it, while Eily, who always believed
I really was, would howl the place down, and Anne would join
in for company. Then Honor and Maureen took to book-binding
in their sitting-room, to professional standards, and the whole of
the upper part of the house stank of fish glue . . . While my mother
was living in Florence she had had favourite books beautifully
bound in vellum with her initials on, and it was this that started
them off. Maureen had always loved books, not so much the
legends and swashbuckling high romance that appealed most to
Eily and me but gentler fiction and the letters of real people,
Mme de Sévigné, Horace Walpole, Stevenson, and Gertrude

Bell—inspired by Fitzie, the latter, and she had started to teach herself Arabic.

This new passion for the form of books themselves completed the taste that turned her a few years later into a bookseller for life. Harry Batsford was a friend of my father's and, when she thought she would like publishing, started her off in the bookshop of his firm to learn first what he considered the essential element of publishing, an appreciation of public taste. Maureen instantly fell in love with the public, and could never be persuaded to leave the shop for the publishing offices. Socially very shy in ordinary life, in a bookshop she found what she called 'an adequate reason for meeting people', and became everybody's friend. She loved her customers, particularly the more eccentric ones, and demanding ones who alarmed her colleagues. Batsford's had always specialised in architecture and builders' subjects, and forty years later Maureen was still looking after, with passionate interest, the needs of architectural students who were the grandsons of her original clients. She became such an expert that while still quite young she was given *carte blanche* to keep a couple of Schools of Architecture in foreign universities up to date with their English language books. When Batsford's sold their bookshop to Bumpus her services were considered an essential part of the deal, as they were when Bumpus sold out to Hatchard's, by which time she had become equally expert on art books and collectors' subjects. She kept voluminous notebooks of the special interests of customers all over the world, with remarks in the margin to remind her what the ones she rarely saw were like: 'orange hair', 'limpy', 'bat squeak' or 'boom'. When some Japanese tourists were found to have left behind what was obviously a treasured collection of postcard mementos of their travels and no address, she went to infinite trouble to trace them, and received a letter of thanks addressed simply to: 'The Old Kind Lady, Hatchard's Bookshop,

My mother with Honor and Brendan, 1906

DERRYNANE
(Above) Honor, Brendan, Maureen, 1914
(Below) Bridget and Maureen, 1916

Piccadilly.' Gentle and witty, she was more like my father than any of us, and like him she was loved.

Like all good things, Forty came to an end. In the fifties the Council requisitioned our end of St George's Square and four acres of the back streets behind it to build a comprehensive school. Reasonably cheap flats and bed-sitters, of which there were many in the area, were unavailable anywhere else within walking distance for the staffs of West End restaurants, theatres and clubs, who often left their work after the last buses and underground trains had gone. We therefore felt justified (our own devotion to Forty would hardly have been excuse enough) in mounting a campaign against its demolition. When other appeals had failed, my father brought his old skills into play. He arranged public meetings, addressed the streets for support with a megaphone, standing up in Eily's vintage 1926 open Riley, with her retriever, who refused to be left out, sitting very upright on the back seat. We wanted him to wear his 'runcible hat', which was guaranteed to attract a crowd, but he judged it unsuitable. He had posters printed and stuck on cardboard for people to hang on their railings bearing such slogans as '20 PEOPLE LIVE HERE' and 'QUEEN ELIZABETH never SLEPT HERE but we do'. We would, I think, have got useful publicity if the date of our campaign had not coincided with a newspaper strike. The school was built for 2,500 children, many of whom came over the bridges from Lambeth and Vauxhall in the morning rush hour, and who terrorised the district so that the shops in our village street refused to serve them. We moved to a house in Thurloe Square which thought it was a carbon copy of Forty in South Kensington, with a better, because street level, back garden. But the chimes of Big Ben, and the bugle calls from Chelsea Barracks, and the River with its prenatal influences were far away; and Eily considered the district 'a damned suburb'. There could never be another Forty.

Books

'We must,' said my mother, 'have provided the most curious assortment of books imaginable to half the hotel libraries of Europe.' When she arrived with her parents, such libraries usually contained a few guide books and local histories for loan to guests, and a motley collection of the sort of books, in various languages, that guests had had no further use for and had left behind, usually novels brought along for the journey. Never were there any children's books. Her father went through books, my mother said, like an express train that had got behind its schedule. He could not possibly have dragged round Europe all the books he bought, and as he had a photographic, encyclopaedic memory, he wouldn't have wanted to keep most of them anyway. Occasionally he would leave a little cache of books he did want to keep, but not to travel with, to be held for him by someone with whom he had struck up an aquaintance in the town, but mostly he shed them 'like leaves in Vallombrosa', and they would find their way into the hotel library. Occasionally, coming to that hotel again, my mother would find them (hunting desperately for something readable), and would be embarrassed: what must other guests have made meanwhile of her father's habit of getting into heated arguments with the author in the margins? If his (frequently ribald) comments were in pencil she would rub them out, but all too often they were in ink, in his strong, distinctive and beautifully legible hand: 'Idiot!' or even '*Merde!*' or '*Stronzo!*' were his most frequent protests, words not heard in polite society and which he would never have used before her. She would look them up in the appropriate dictionary, and then black them out very carefully in equally dark ink, lest people should think her beloved father was not nice at all. 'You should *never* write in a book,' we were told, 'even, to relieve your feelings, in invisible ink.'

There were lending libraries in the larger towns, and in Paris, Florence and Rome there were English Reading Rooms; but here again children were not catered for. Books were bought for her, mostly classical legends or those of whatever country they were in, and these she would come to know almost by heart before she would be driven again to reading the detritus left by grown-ups in the hotel library. My grandmother's blindness made my mother the best reader-aloud I have ever known. It is, except for professionals on the radio, a lost art now. Even when some of us were quite grown up, we used to sit around as a family, the girls sewing, my father and brother smoking, while my mother read to us. Our particular delight were the works of Amanda McKitterick Ros, a sketchily self-educated Edwardian novelist, wife of the station master at Larne, with a passion for alliteration which my mother used oh-so-gently to over-stress, and for such splendid descriptions of emotional states as 'the blackened ball of sorrow rose in her throat', which would throw the whole family into hysterics.

Never having had (except as a baby) a proper nursery of her own, she provided us with one with the greatest conventional care, with a Norland Institute trained children's nurse, not called Nanny but Nurse Margaret (who became Marmie, and upon whom we doted), and a nursery maid called Winifred (known as Wee Wee) to do all the real work of the nursery and leave Marmie

(83)

free to play with us, and teach us paper-folding, and doll's dress-making, and all the other Montessori method skills. We loved these, but what we always wanted was more stories.

These were provided when, properly washed and brushed and without our pinafores, we were brought down to the back drawing-room after tea. Often there were stories at bedtime, too.

'Legends,' my mother told me later, 'have survived the centuries because they are the best stories—otherwise they'd have bored people and been forgotten.' Pandora's Box, Cadmus and the Dragon's Teeth, and the finding of the Golden Fleece, were interspersed with German, Norse, and (particularly) French and Italian tales. We liked the serials best, when the same characters would turn up day after day, from the Wanderings of Ulysses to the stories of the Niebelungen, and the adventures of Finn and Cuchulain. These latter, the great Irish legends, she had come to herself when she was grown up, and had fallen in love first with Irish and then with my father, and I thought she told those best of all; but to my youngest sister she never told these, and it was Eily and I who passed them on to Anne, for Anne was born in 1923, and by then the Irish Romance was over and had ended in violence, tragedy, and the destruction of all that my father had worked for, and my mother put Ireland behind her.

She always told stories with a book in her hand, even though she knew them by heart, showing us pictures in it if there were any. 'When you were small,' she told me later, 'it was quite often just any book about anything that I had handy: but it was to give you the idea that stories came from books, that books were treasure-trove.' Reading was, for us as babies, a treat in store for when we were older, the magic key to all the stories in the world. My father, it seemed to me, led a wonderful life, for he read a great deal and always, I presumed, stories. One day when I climbed on his knee and looked at his book, I didn't recognise any of the letters of which by then I knew quite a few. 'It's Greek,' he explained, and my mother said, 'Daddy has lots of keys to open books with, he can read about Ulysses in Greek and Finn and Cuchulain in Irish, the languages they talked in. You wait! You can learn to read quite soon now.'

We could all of us read by the time we were five. Marmie was never allowed to teach us, in spite of all her Norland training, for my mother felt passionately that children could be retarded by reading being made into a lesson, and only if she taught us herself could she be sure it would always be regarded as a treat. The alphabet learned by rote she considered an invention of the devil. 'It's stupid, it doesn't mean anything, letters must belong in words to a child or it's mindless torture.' We learned by the phonetic method, then very new. Combinations like 'th' were known as tricks—'Shall I show you a new trick?'—or 'silly English', because she considered that Italian, spelt exactly as it was pronounced, was the only really sensible language. Neither she nor anyone else ever succeeded in teaching me to spell.

We were never allowed to 'play reading' for long on end, and she always stopped well before we were bored. She came up to the nursery specially to teach whichever of us was at the learning stage, never at the same time each day, so that it was always a surprise and a treat to have her all to oneself to play at it with. We had *Reading without Tears*, then about the only book available for the purpose: 'a cat sat on a mat . . . Nan has a bat . . .' but also we learned by cards. Playing cards with letters on them had not then been invented, but my mother had adapted an ordinary pack for the purpose by sticking paper with a letter (and later a word) on each. If you could guess the 'noise' the letter should make (and later what the word was) you got the cards, if not she did; and whoever got the most cards won. The triumph when you 'beat Mummy at reading' with the whole pack! Years later, when

I lived in Rome and my char brought her baby to work with her every morning, I taught the child to read in no time by playing with Scrabble letters, and sympathised with my mother over how much longer it must have taken her with 'silly English' spelling.

Writing we learned as a kind of drawing. We would play at drawing houses or animals or people for a little while, and then my mother would say, 'Can you draw a C for cat under your cat?' She hated a cramped handwriting, and believed that a child would write more freely if it regarded it as drawing. Later when we were writing easily she would sometimes slip a slim ivory letter-opener under one's hand: if the blade wouldn't pass, it showed you were leaning on your wrist. 'You should write with your whole hand running along like a mouse across the page, not just fingers,' she would say, and teach you to lean your forearm, half way up, on the edge of the table, and swoop your hand about making circles and flourishes freely all over the page before you drew, equally freely, a letter or a word. For the same reason, she never let us write on lined paper until we had acquired the habit of writing properly, believing that lines cramped a child who should enjoy first the letters as beautiful things.

I had already been shown the early illuminated manuscripts in the British Museum for the sake of the pictures in them when my mother took me further along the gallery to show me late ones with more modern scripts, to enjoy their beauty. We had a very good painting book at home, with initial letters taken from the Book of Kells and designed for children to colour. The Celtic interlacing patterns inside the letters were great fun to do, and started me off on a passion for illuminating manuscripts of my own. When I was about fourteen I secretly made at school what I called The Boland Book of Hours for my mother's birthday. It took so long that I only finished one of the Hours, the evening Hour of Compline, but I knew that was her favourite and luckily started with it. It was a bit of a muddle, as each page was decorated in a different style that I admired, from Celtic through early French to late Florentine, and the scripts were Gothic here and Italian there; but never mind, she burst into tears of pleasure when I gave it to her. The only other time I ever made her cry was when I came downstairs from my bedroom in my first grown-up evening dress, for my first dance, and she stood in tears on the drawing-room landing. I thought I must look hideous, but she said, 'It's just if only Father and Mother were here to see you!'

Books always led on to something else. When I was reading a historical novel I was taken to the London Museum to see the few costumes they then had of the period (the Victoria and Albert had none in those days), or to the Tower of London to see the weapons and armour, or to a house where the characters could have lived—anything real to make the fiction more vivid. If a place was mentioned that could be easily reached from London and could be guaranteed still to look right, we would go there—just for a glance, never too long, for children are quickly bored. She might have done all these things before with the older children, she certainly did them again for Eily and Anne: each child was separate, special, and there was only one right moment for everything with each.

So long as I could get at the story, I didn't mind. The nuns at school (the same one at Roehampton, where my mother had ended up as Head of the School, and where the nuns were still devoted to her) took her advice on this point in the library, though their rules were stricter. On Sundays and Thursdays there we were allowed books out of the normally locked 'Classics' cupboard—Jane Austen, Dickens, Thackeray, Scott and such; on Feast Days and Holidays we were allowed 'story books' from another locked cupboard; but novels of any nun-acceptable kind in any language were left on the open shelves.

When you could read, what could you read? Absolutely anything. No books were ever forbidden in the house except novels in translation (my mother was terrified lest we grew up monolingual). An exception was made for novels in Russian, but those were only allowed in French translations, which she considered better than the English ones then available.

She rightly believed that if books were forbidden they would be got at and devoured with an eye to 'what could be wrong in them'. You could never be too young to read something—what you weren't ready to know would go over your head anyway; but you could easily be too old, lose the pleasure of reading it at the age when you might have enjoyed it most, and discover things which, if you had read them earlier and, uninterested, left them in your subconscious, would not now startle and intrigue you.

Reading, with my mother, was what would nowadays be called an 'on-going' process (horrible word). When she read aloud to me when I was small, she always sat me on her knee, following the lines with her finger (helping to give me the idea that stories could be had at will by reading lines in books). When she stopped reading (always at a cliff-hanging point) she would say, 'What do you suppose could possibly happen next?' Next time she read from the book she would ask me what I'd guessed. This was on the principle of the child in one of Kipling's stories who, when his mother wasn't able to finish a story she was reading at bedtime, found that it came out of his own head all new and exciting 'just as if he'd read it in a book'. Then she would read on; but my guesses were my first attempts at fiction-mongering on my own account. I was encouraged to draw pictures about the story, we dressed up like characters in it, with an older or a younger sister I play-acted scenes out of it. As I grew older, we would talk endlessly with my mother about the books we were reading.

I was fortunate, as the fourth member of the family, in that there were already a wealth of children's books in the house by the time I was ready for them. We were all fortunate in that my father had been given as a twenty-first birthday present a life sub-scription to the London Library, from which a member can have out ten books at a time in London and fifteen at a time elsewhere. 'The best investment ever made,' he said, 'I educated six children with it.' We used to go in with my mother and be allowed to choose one book each while she got hers and my father's. One day when I went into the Library some years ago and saw old Mr Cox, the chief assistant who must have been then in his eighties, still in his place though I had read that he was retiring, I told him how glad I was that he hadn't gone yet. 'It would be the end of an era.' 'Oh no,' he said, 'the era that mattered ended when the last of the Bolands had read the last of the G. A. Henty's.'

My mother's personal predilection was for letters and memoirs. 'They're like stories,' she told me, 'because you get to know the people like you do characters in fiction, far better than in ordinary history books.' She led me early to Mme de Sévigné's letters, and the memoirs of court ladies of the reigns of Louis XIV and XV, via historical novels which had given me the settings of the periods; to my sister Maureen, with gentler and less flamboyant tastes, she had given first the letters of R. L. Stevenson, which I didn't like so much. Maureen had come to share her devotion to Horace Walpole's letters—to which I became so addicted that a friend of my own age got quite worried, saying I was obsessed with my beloved Horry. My mother took both Maureen and me, in turn at the right age, to Strawberry Hill, to see his house. My first printed 'Work' was a prize-winning entry at fifteen in a *New Statesman* competition for a letter in his style, and my first novel, when I was twenty-one, was written in the form of 18th-century letters.

A family friend was Miss Emma Austen Leigh, who was as

(89)

obsessed with her Great Aunt Jane as ever I came to be with Horace Walpole. She used to worry my mother dreadfully by giving us all exams from time to time on what she always called reverently The Works, with questions (like 'What was Mr Darcy's Christian name, and where are the two places where it is mentioned') rather like those set now in 'Mastermind' on the television. My sister Eily, who was her godchild and got more exams than the rest of us, never could like The Works, and my mother said, 'it's Emma's fault. A child's pleasure in a book is such a delicate plant—if you force it, and overwater it, it dies.'

I think that the most heroic part of my mother's devotion to our upbringing was her self-sacrifice over books in the summer holidays. In the (in those days) tiny fishing village of Wissant in Picardy where we rented the same little house for three months every year for ten years for the sake of our French and our health, there was of course no bookshop or library. There was the safest possible bathing, with miles and miles of slowly shelving sandy beach; there was also a tennis club for my father and the older children. But there was nothing whatever for my mother to do except read. Each of us six children was allowed to bring two books from the London Library. They had to be chosen with care. The first proviso was that no-one should have read them before; the second was that each choice should be legible at a pinch by the next older and the next younger child. That left three books between the parents. My father gallantly maintained that he would have no time for anything but bathing, tennis and a newspaper if it rained. My mother tried to drag her three books out by teaching herself astronomy and Greek, and even at one point tried Russian (but abandoned it saying that learning a living language from a book without someone to talk to was a waste of time). She borrowed books from M le Curé and all the villas just along the coast, she read all her own books and finally fell back on crossword puzzles, books of which were beginning to be published. We left nothing in Wissant every year but our bathing things (her secret hope being, I think, that we should weary of it), and what a library, she often sighed, we could have built up, if only we had known from the beginning we should always be coming back!

Why my mother never wrote herself I shall never know, unless it was that she was a perfectionist and would never have been satisfied with anything she had written. Her father as a young man had published a good deal of verse, including a set of Petrarchan sonnets called *Ad Inuptam* when he was courting my grandmother which are included in several anthologies of Australian poetry. We thought them dreadfully funny (apart from feeling that it was almost improper for people to write love poems to one's grandmother), particularly one which ended—

And overhead the Southern Cross did shine
Like that which blazed o'er conquering Constantine.

Perhaps the fact that we laughed at them (she was a-critical on that one subject herself) made my mother all the more reluctant to try her own hand at writing. She did once think of compiling a phrase book for Catholic travellers who wanted to go to confession abroad, to be called 'How to Sin in Four Languages' (after she'd been approached shyly by an English woman tourist in the village church), and we all had a hilarious time contributing improbable sins; and she did make a new translation from the Latin of the Nuptial Mass, because she said that the existing one was enough to put young people off matrimony, which was published; but as far as I know that was all.

Wissant

———⊃₀⊖₀⊂———

I have never known anyone who could make herself so much at home in a train as my mother, as a result of a childhood forever on the move. She always 'travelled light', but from a small amount of hand-luggage would emerge an amazing paraphernalia of collapsible comforts. There were always two very light cashmere rugs (two light ones were much warmer than one heavy one, her father had explained); they were rolled sausage-wise, bound with two straps with a handle between. Inside were a number of small sausages. One was of oil cloth containing a bundle of little light rods which slotted and screwed together in a trice into the framework of a little table whose top was the oilcloth, that clipped across it so rigidly that you could use it to play or even to write on. Another had once been a knitting bag but now held a minute double pack of patience cards, a little pencil case full of a row of tiny marbles and a collapsible wire frame that opened out to hold them for solitaire; lonely games for a lonely child, these, but a third sausage was a little chinese reed mat painted in squares rolled round two tubes, one containing a rouleau of gambling chips to be used for draughts and another full of dice—always enough of them to allow for loss under the seats. The last sausage was two air cushions, a square one to sit on, an oblong one for your head, rolled round a little pump, and a tortoiseshell tube about four and a half inches long which, when you pressed its base, opened into a little circular fan of very thin tortoiseshell blades that you pumped with your thumb for hot summer journeys.

In an overnight bag there travelled a little feather-light aluminium saucepan about four inches across and three inches deep, with hinged handles that folded round it. It had a lid which you removed, to lift out first a little fine-filigree walnut whose two halves were hinged (to insert just enough tea for one cup) and which hung on a little chain from a ring for dunking it; next a little circular aluminium stand fractionally smaller than the saucepan, for the latter to stand on with a slightly raised base on which one placed two little flat white cakes, like continental sugar lumps, of a solid fuel called 'meta'. The first thing my mother did on arriving in an hotel was to inspect her washbasin, for only in this would she brew up tea: if it was of the space-saving semicircular kind, without a round flat bottom on which to stand the little stove, the hotel was given a black mark and never used again. Foreigners, no matter how good the hotel, never made tea properly. But the meta stove was a modern invention, and in her own childhood the family's travelling stove had been a minute but elaborate paraffin one, which alas I never saw, and the safety precaution of using the washbasin to stand it in was probably a very necessary one, with my mother as a little girl lighting it for blind Gran.

She carried a 'First Aid Kit'. This was a little padded oblong oiled silk bag of a beautiful shade of peacock blue. It contained a small bottle of eau de cologne and a separately oiled-silk-rolled set of tiny squares of cotton pre-soaked in some kind of emollient oil; these would be liberally sprinkled with eau de cologne and used to wipe the face and hands before one arrived anywhere, for soap and water were no match for the mixture of oil and soot which, she maintained, railway companies spread everywhere like butter. These little squares were put in another oiled silk bag for the contents to be disposed of later and 'not, darling, *not* thrown out of the window! Think of the poor natives!' The First Aid Kit otherwise contained only a small hip flask, with an inscription announcing that it had been won by my father for athletics at his prep school, from which we were all liberally dosed with brandy before channel crossings—as a result of which practice I have never been able to touch brandy at any other time. My mother was an appalling sailor, and when travelling from Australia at the age of eight had been found leaning out of a porthole pouring her mother's expensive hair oil into the sea, having heard the expression 'pouring oil on troubled waters'.

Travelling, for us, meant chiefly the going backwards and forwards to Ireland until 1918, when I was five, and thereafter, apart from rare trips for special reasons, the general exodus of the whole family for the summer. In our early days the house in St George's Square would be closed, after deliciously expectant days when huge trunks with domed lids stood open in every bedroom and we clattered with exciting echoes up and down stone stairs whose carpets had been taken up and sent to be cleaned. After the cats had at last been rounded up and stuffed, protesting, into their travelling baskets and the canaries always almost forgotten, I can just remember, before a fleet of taxis became inevitable, the parents departing in a hansom for the station while the children and nurses were packed with the livestock and some of the luggage in one 'four-wheeler' and the servants and the rest of the luggage in another, the roofs of both vehicles piled high with trunks. For three years we rented furnished every summer a sprawling Victorian rectory at Lockinge in Berkshire, and then, my mother beginning to worry about our French, Wissant was discovered.

Wissant was a little village on the coast half way between

Boulogne and Calais. It has now become, I believe, a 'resort', with hotels and a casino and the devil knows what, but in those days it consisted of a few fishermen's houses, a church, three shops, a mill and the hopefully-called Hotel des Bains, which was an inn with sanded floors, a dining-room with one long table, and perhaps a dozen bedrooms.

Beside the hotel a bridge crossed a little river which fed the millpond, and across this bridge and round behind a fisherman's cottage was the house of Mme Noël. The back parts, which for practical purposes were the front, looked like a small farmhouse in a large walled kitchen garden; the (official) front had been given perhaps fifty years before the look of what my mother called 'the sort of house Eugénie Grandet lived in', with bright green shutters, and stained glass panels in the front door decorated with wrought iron to which ran a brick tiled path. On this side the nine foot garden wall was replaced with tall wrought iron railings for a short distance in front of the house; but I never saw either the gate in them or the front door itself opened. All traffic to and from the house was through a wooden door in the wall round one side, above which dangled a shop bell which jangled as the door was opened, for the produce of the garden, the only one in the village, was for sale. The hotel used it as a sort of annex, renting rooms from the Noëls when necessary for extra guests, who would cross the bridge to the hotel for meals. We took the whole house, except for the corner where the Noëls lived, having lunch and dinner at the hotel—and for ten years we spent the whole of every summer there, and some of us often spent Easter there as well.

The Pas de Calais is really quite dreadfully dull. As flat as Holland, treeless, hedgeless, featureless rectangles of patchwork-quilt fields spread to the sea in one direction and to the horizon in all others. Through Wissant ran the Boulogne-Calais coast road, with a fork beyond the village where a side road ran inland to the market town of Marquise, so you could go for a walk left, right, or in one direction sideways, but there was not so much as a track elsewhere on which you could tread without stepping on somebody's crops. The only hump in the landscape was Caesar's Camp, the circular earthwork thrown up when the Romans were preparing for the invasion of England at this the narrowest point in the Channel. Even the sides, the moat-like ditches and that flat top of the earth were cultivated, and though we played there it was at our peril from an angry farmer.

What Wissant had for the family was mile after mile of wonderful sands and dead safe bathing for the little ones, and extremely good tennis for my father and the older children. The presence of the latter amenity was explained by the existence, a little way from the village itself, of a row of about a dozen big villas along the dunes above the sea and the (usually almost empty) Hotel de la Digue, of greater pretensions than the Hotel des Bains in the village. The villas stood, without gardens or even grass around them, growing straight out of the sand, each the product of a different architectural frenzy but all with bay windows here and lancet windows there and pepper-pot turrets everywhere and mansard roofs with gargoyles on them. In and out of them tumbled dozens of children of the rich bourgeoisie of Roubaix and Lille to play with us and race sand yachts on the miles of beach, and young people to provide tennis partners for the older Bolands. The *digue* was some 70 yards of esplanade, beginning and ending in sand where the hopeful turn-of-the-century speculators had given up the attempt to make another Wimereux here and departed. But meanwhile a clubhouse and some admirable hard courts had been supplied by the textile-rich bourgeois of Roubaix and Lille who sent their enormous families every summer.

Looking back, I cannot imagine how my mother stood it, but

Bridget, Maureen, Brendan, Honor: Derrynane 1916

Maureen, Bridget, Brendan in the garden at Forty, 1918

WISSANT, 1925
M and Mme Noël

Right to left : Brendan, Honor, Maureen, Bridget, Eily, Anne

at the time it never occurred to me that she didn't adore the place
as much as everyone else. She didn't play tennis. The younger
ones had a nurse, or later a governess, to look after them on the
beach. She read, went for walks, and when the beach and sand
dunes palled we went with her. It was then that we learned the
games she used to play with her father, tramping the country
roads of more beautiful parts of France, of Italy, Germany and
Switzerland. There was 'I Spy'—with mighty little to spy, but
somehow she taught us to find tiny wild flowers, ferns and different kinds of grasses in the narrow ditches and verges between the
roads and the crops. We 'spied' them in English (score one) and
French (score two), and we took what we couldn't identify home
to look up, particularly the grasses, of which we made a remarkable collection over the years. We played 'Quotations', finding apt
ones to describe what we passed, or the better variation of it
called 'Up from the meadows'. This consisted of making up a
story entirely from quotations. This had started in my mother's
own childhood with the opening of *Barbara Fretchie*: 'Up from
the meadows rich with corn'. The peak of this game was considered to have been reached when my youngest sister, Anne, then
six years old and considered really too young to play, capped
somebody's quotation from Sassoon: 'Good morning, good
morning, the general said,' with a line from A. A. Milne: 'And
he upped with his battle-axe and blipped him on the head.'

Then there was 'Houses': what kind of a house would you
build if someone gave you that piece of land, just there? Exactly
what would it look like, what sort of roof and doors and windows
would it have? Would it have shutters (a very Wissantaise feature),
or blinds, or neither? Which way would it face, the windows of
which rooms would look out on what part of the view? My houses
were always built round courtyards, known as 'Dooka's Quiet
Insides' (my nickname was Dooka). Eily's always had a great

many stables 'with a tower with a clock on top'. Maureen's were architecturally fascinating, and she would passionately reject additions we offered in 'the wrong style for *that* house'. To the houses game we added 'Gardens', and on this I became hooked. In bed at night I would play 'Gardens' by myself, and have done so ever since. They became so detailed and real to me that once, not long ago, talking about gardens with some friends who knew my proclivity and some other guests who didn't, I said: 'I have a garden like this . . .; and then I have another one like this . . . ' After I had left, one of the other guests asked our host whether 'that woman's' marvellous gardens were open to the public. 'She lives,' he said, 'in London, and has one garden, twenty-two foot square.'

It was my mother who, on one of her further-afield walks, discovered the Ségars' chateau. It had a stream and a wood. Firmly she asked to see the owner. Her children, she said, spent the whole of every summer without sight of a tree. They adored Wissant, but might she bring them sometimes to picnic in the wood? The Ségars implored her to tell her children to regard the wood as their own—which, thereafter, we did. It was a long walk for short legs, but we had got to know the farmers round about and they would tell us when a car or a cart was going in that direction and we would pile in, getting a lift one way at least. It was the most wonderful wood in the world, with the stream running in a deep gully, with on one side 'Indian Pathway' and on the other side 'Spider's Track'. When some fifty years later Maureen and I found our present house in Hampshire we bought it largely, I think, because it had almost just such a wood, with a stream in a gully.

When it rained, which (surely more often than I remember?) it sometimes did even in Wissant, we younger ones played in the *buanderie*, which we called the *bu*, the wash-house built away from the house in an angle of the garden wall, with a huge boiler and copper used particularly for the annual *grand lessive*, when Charlotte-from-over-the-way came to help Mme Noël, and every stitch of linen in the house was washed and spread out to bleach on the sand dunes. Here, on the huge white-scrubbed table in the middle, used for the ironing, we would play cards, notably *bouchon*. This was an improved version of Snap, taught us by some of the 'villa children': a cork from a wine bottle stood in the middle of the table, and, when two cards of the same value were turned up, instead of crying 'Snap'! everyone grabbed for it. Finger-nails were examined before this game was played, and anyone whose nails were adjudged too long was sent to cut them. My mother, as Eily once remarked, was 'awfully good at rain', and knew a lot of games for bad weather, most of them taught her by kindly ladies who had taken pity on the little girl sitting alone in the corners of hotel lounges in her childhood. The best of these were infinite varieties of paper folding and cutting, including origami and one now marketed as 'Tangrams'. We drew and cut out paper dolls, and made and painted complete wardrobes to dress them in (with little folding flaps of paper over the shoulders and round the waists). When we got bored with contemporary dresses for them she showed us how to turn them into knights in armour and their ladies, Robin Hood characters, kings and queens and courtiers of different periods. We made paper houses, and once, carried away after a visit to St Omer not far away, we built a whole cathedral propped up inside with books, complete with flying buttresses and stained-glass windows made of toffee papers. Then she would give prizes for designing jackets for our favourite books, and for illustrating the stories. The fact that none of us except Anne were much good added to the entertainment.

There was very little excitement in the village. The only

transport, apart from the fish lorries that came every morning to take the catch of the half dozen boats to Boulogne or Calais for Paris, was George's bus, that went twice a week to Calais. George was an Englishman who, as a soldier in the 1914–18 War, married a local girl. He was reputed to have poured paraffin over his mother-in-law, who owned the grocer's shop, and set fire to her, but with no lasting results. The engine of his bus had been originally, everyone said, that of the German submarine whose wreck could still be seen at low tide. My brother, who examined it with interest, confirmed the probability of this. Occasionally a special bus would stop in the village while taking English tourists for a trip along the coast road, they having landed at one port in the morning and intending to return home from the other that night. We always hid, or someone in the village would be sure to pounce on us for explanations of what the poor creatures wanted. It was in fact always tea, and we knew from experience that they wouldn't like what they would be offered at the hotel—and there was nowhere else. We were sorry for them, for it was a very dull road, and my mother, having her own strong views on tea, every year brought over an immense packet of Lipton's as a gift to the hotel for their benefit, and had explained about thin bread and butter, and about jam being different from *compôte de fruit*; but we were bitterly ashamed of them, and stressed heavily that we were Irish and quite different. This, the village assured us politely, saw itself, but we could at least speak their language and find out why they were so cross. They behaved abominably. In the 'twenties the exchange was heavily in the pound's favour, and in Calais, we had often heard, they used to throw their small change over the ship's side onto the quays before they left for the natives to scramble for; when one bus load, who were at least good tempered, did this in the village as they were leaving, a group of fisherboys, lounging on the bridge, picked the coins up and flung them back into their faces at close range. One group flung the beautiful crusty slices of bread on the hotel floor and ground it in with their heels to express their disgust, and they would often fish out the tea bags that preceded my mother's gifts of Lipton's and fling them out of the window in their rage. Another scene of violence occurred one Sunday outside the church, where a bus load were appalled to see all the little girls who were going down to the beach after High Mass pulling their dresses off over their heads as they came down the steps and revealing the bathing dresses they wore underneath and tossing them, with their Sunday hats, to waiting relatives, while the little boys wriggled out of their shirts and trousers. The English rushed forward and boxed the ears of any they could catch, while my mother tried to explain to their indignant parents about the Non-conformist Conscience, failing until she hit on the idea of saying that they didn't approve of wine either, which so paralysed the natives with amazement that the bus load got away fairly intact. But Wissant certainly made no contribution to the *entente cordiale*.

Peculiarly disliked at one period by the natives was the *Continental Daily Mail*, an edition of the paper printed, I imagine, in Paris. It used to fly a plane up and down along the coast spoiling the heavens with hideous sky-writing advertisements; but one year the paper delighted my heart. They ran a competition at all the resorts along the northern coast for the best sandcastles made by children. As our Mayor had written a particularly virulent objection to the sky-writing they included Wissant as a 'resort' as a gesture of goodwill, though the handful of visitors it could house and its lack of any amenities for their entertainment scarcely merited the honour. I considered myself a dab at the art, and I needed the money: I wanted a particularly splendid kite to be had at the village general store. No humdrum castle for me; I decided to overpower the judges with a magnificently sculptured tomb, with the figures of a crusader and his lady lying atop with their little dog at their feet. The village was shocked to the core: hovering on the sand dunes above the beach so as not to seem to give support to the hated *Daily Mail*, they could not see the finer points of my work, it seemed to them to represent a man and woman in bed together (with the hump of a stone hot-water bottle at their feet), absolutely not a suitable subject for a little girl to choose. As a matter of fact I had to explain what it did represent to the judges, but I won the prize. As I crossed the bridge over the millstream to the shop I tore off as usual a leaf from the tall bullrushes that overtopped it for the delicious feeling of tearing its crispness, and, my mind aloft with the coveted kite I was on my way to buy, I shredded the precious note in my hand as well. Even the pangs of unrequited love in later years were not more bitter than my grief when I saw what I had done. Although my father, still laughing over the village's reaction to my masterpiece, which had been reported to him at the tennis courts, made good the loss, and it proved the best kite ever seen on the beach, it still hurts me to think of that lost note.

As I grew older the bridge figured largely in my life, for we had to cross it on the way from our house to the hotel for dinner, and, congenitally late in getting changed and clean, I often missed the family exodus and had to cross it alone, running the gauntlet of the whistling fisher-lads who sat on either side of it every night. I can date my reaching womanhood from the night when, at fifteen, I took my time instead of scuttling, reciting to myself a poem I had recently discovered:

> Accours, jeune Chromis, je t'aime et je suis belle,
> Blanche comme Diane et légère comme elle;

Comme elle grande, et fière, et les bergers, le soir,
Lorsque les yeux baissés je passe sans les voir,
Regardent après moi et disent: 'Comme elle est belle!'

That same year I entered a fancy dress competition at the hotel as a Greek Maiden, joining two bath towels together down the sides, sewing a Greek key-pattern along the bottom in purple ribbon, crossing more purple ribbon under my breasts, threading still more into my rope-soled beach shoes and cross-gartering it up the legs, and dressing my too-much hair inexpertly in what I hoped was a Greek style on top of my head. I dragooned my brother into escorting me, insisting on his going in costume too, so he, who was six foot four by then, draped himself in two sheets, picked one of M Noël's blood-red roses and pinned it in the middle of the snowy expanse, on his stomach, and announced he was the Last Rose of Summer. The lads on the bridge cheered wildly that night. The French judges missed the English point of my brother's outfit, but I won another prize and a dreadful middle-aged Scot at the hotel made a pass at me. That was a great summer.

The principal regular excitement every year was the *Ducasse*. This was the feast of the Dedication of the church. The steam organ of a merry-go-round blared gloriously all day and night in the *place* beside the church, there were jugglers and tumblers and, every year, a dog called Johnnie ('Allez-oop, Johnnie!') who jumped through a hoop. One year there was a minute little girl who squeezed as though boneless through a tiny barrel, to the distress of my mother, particularly when I borrowed a barrel from M Noël, only slightly larger, and tried to do the same thing with my own plump person, with the inevitable result that the barrel had to be dismantled from around me. In the evening the bus would be shunted out of its garage and a dance was held, with a fiddler, two accordions and a tambourine, vying with and in

(103)

close proximity to the steam organ. It was all glorious, except tea-time, when we all had to sit round the big table in the *buanderie* and Mme Noël brought in the *Ducasse* cake, a cartwheel of solidified custard soaked in rum, and we all had to eat some with cries of delight until she went away proudly content and we could bury the rest in a flower bed. The other occasion when she always treated us was on the third day of the *grand lessive*, when, the work complete, the Noëls and Charlotte-from-over-the-way and other neighbours ate vast quantities of *beignets*. They were served in batches of eighteen, and at intervals Mme Noël would poke her head round the corner of the house and shout to the *bu* '*Encore dixhuit?*' and we would chorus eagerly, '*Encore, toujours encore, Madame!*' to her delight.

M Noël remains forever my idea of a gardener. Silent, shy, from dawn till dark he was at his work. The rest of the village was pure silvery sea sand, but M Noël's soil was as rich as chocolate. His particular pride were his dahlias, as big as soup plates, growing near the outside lavatory (we had no indoor sanitation, nor electricity, and water only from a pump). Only to my youngest sister, Anne, did he talk much. At two or three she would stump round the garden after him, delighting to pick off snails and earwigs and chattering away in a language they, miraculously, both understood. The rest of us all grew up with a tinge of the local accent to our French, to my mother's despair, but Anne and my brother, who went out a lot with the fishermen, spoke pure Walloon forever more.

Other figures from those days haunt my memory: one is Guibert. When we first knew Wissant he used to appear as a sort of beadle at the church on Sundays and for processions on feast days, known as the Suisse because his uniform was founded on that of the Swiss Guard of the French Monarchy. He also acted as Town Crier, going round the village with a drum, announcing such things as dogs or property lost, or the annual arrival of the strolling players who would perform *La Dame aux Caméllias* or *Le Cid* in a barn, to my enraptured satisfaction. He seemed to me very tall and splendid, but over the years he shrank even faster than I grew, and at last he was forcibly retired and, with the march of progress, never replaced. He had been too often too drunk for even his not very onerous duties, and from shortage of funds took to meths instead of wine. He was found one morning in the stream just behind our house, drowned, where he had fallen, in four inches of water. I still think of him when I see the phrase 'How are the mighty fallen', for to me even in his decay he had the air of such an important man.

Another was M Tire, a retired army officer to whom my mother sent me in hope of eradicating my Walloon accent. I had to read aloud to him, and he kindly chose books he thought suitable to my years, such as Daudet's *Lettres de mon Moulin*; but he always fell asleep, understandably, almost at once, and the mere sight of a Daudet on a shelf still summons up for me his stentorian snores. My mother, who knew he could use the money for my session with him, lent me a collection of Maupassant short stories and the suggestion that I should read those.

He was shocked, but he had never read them, and sat bolt upright throughout and always kept me beyond the hour if we were in the middle of a story: fifteen and seventy shared the excitement of the world's greatest short story writer, and he took to giving me *babas* soaked in rum to encourage me to get my mother to provide another volume when the first should be finished, and I had grown too fond of him to admit that I hated them; and to this day my addiction to Maupassant is tinged with rum.

A third figure is the enigmatic one of Captain Hesketh. Those were the days when a certain easily recognisable type of Englishman was always called Captain, the rank he had achieved during the War, and always wore and often fingered a small moustache. We first met this particular gentleman on the beach, where he was teaching his eighteen-month-old son to swim, which the baby did a great deal better than our five-year-old Anne, who still clung tenaciously to water-wings. He also had a vocabulary enormous for his age, the more remarkable that the words came out in English, French or German, and in another language we presumed was mere baby-talk till Captain Hesketh explained that it was Roumanian, which impressed us so much that we carried him home in triumph to demonstrate his prowess to my mother, Captain Hesketh being necessarily invited to come too. This was the first of many visits the gallant Captain paid to her, expressing unbounded delight in finding in such a cultural wilderness 'someone of his own kind' to talk to. My mother declared herself flattered, and to us admitted that she was intrigued: what on earth was he doing in Wissant all the summer, and how did he earn a living? He had told us that he was practising to swim the channel, and, indeed, he did swim nearly every day back and forth the five miles or so between Cap Blanc Nez and Cap Griz Nez, the point from which the Channel swimmers used to start. But we knew the true breed well: every year one or more of them could be seen around our long bay, immensely fat men and women who would lollop up onto our sands to rest when the tide was in at the capes. But Captain Hesketh was a wiry little man; and the others used often to swim far out towards England with a boat to follow them, which he never did.

At length she wormed his story out of him (for I have come honestly by my passion for listening to strange tales, as they say of hereditary tendencies). During the troubles in Roumania between King Carol and those who pressed for his abdication, Captain Hesketh had worked as an undercover agent, a Rupert of

Hentzau figure in the *Prisoner of Zenda* tradition, by his account of things, but on behalf of the King. The language of the court was German and his German was certainly good enough, my mother said, for him to have worked behind the German lines, as he claimed during the Great War, and passed as a German businessman; Roumanian was quickly learned, he said, by anyone with good French and Italian, which he had. In spite of his efforts, King Carol had recently been deposed in favour of his younger son, Michael, and Captain Hesketh, his wife and baby, and the latter's Roumanian nurse had had to flee the country. He now had a job for the French Royalist movement, working for the restoration of Jean III, the Comte de Paris. Under his cover as an English Channel swimmer studying currents along our bit of the coast, he was working up local support which he hoped would eventually become as strong as it already was in Brittany. My brother on his bicycle used certainly to see his little car driving to neighbouring market towns more frequently than the shopping needs of his little family seemed to warrant: he was recruiting distributors, he told my mother, for the Royalist newspaper, the *Action Française*. My mother developed a theory that he was an *agent provocateur* for the French police, since his cover was so thin that even we children had seen through it. Whichever he was, she doubted if the stolid inhabitants of the Pas de Calais provided fruitful ground for royalist revolution; but poor Captain Hesketh was a born loser. She was just beginning to probe into what his father had done for a living to provide him with his, for an Englishman of his type and period, excellent knowledge of languages, when he and his wife (whom we never got to know beyond a distant wave) and his polyglot baby vanished from the Wissantaise scene overnight, never to return.

What was it that Wissant had for us as children? Many years later when I was living in Rome I met a ghost from those days, one of the 'villa children', of a large family whose surname was Glorieux. The Christian names of the boys, whether because their parents had too little sense of humour or too much for their children's good, were Victor, Hector, Achille and, their classical panache running out, Daniel. The girls were more mercifully called merely Germaine and Gertrude, but perhaps only because they were liable to change their surname anyway. Little Achille had now blossomed into a Monsignor and was working at the Vatican. Wishing more power to his elbow and the hope that there would one day be a Pope Somethingorother *al secolo* Achille Glorieux, I asked him what he thought the magic of Wissant had been. 'I fancy you brought it with you,' he said, 'you were such a *family*.'

Learning
the Facts of Life

There is nothing that many parents find more difficult than what they call 'preparing their children for life'. My mother had no patience with this. 'They hesitate and dither,' she said, 'and leave it too late, or they blush and fuss, and then pretend that sex for people is just like it is for the birds and the bees—the bees, I ask you!' We once had an eighteen-year-old Irish maid in London straight off the bog, who got in a terrible state because she had let a young man kiss her and thought she would inevitably have a baby. 'It was—it was on me mouth, M'm!' she sobbed. My mother considered that what was called innocence was appalling ignorance, the result of criminal neglect, and wrote the girl's mother a furious letter which she was only stopped from posting by my eldest sister who said the mother would probably be worried to death lest we were letting all the unprincipled English kiss her child. 'And if I hadn't luckily noticed she'd been crying,' said my mother, 'she'd have found that she didn't have a baby and would have thought all warnings were nonsense—and next thing you know she'd be having one.'

For a woman born in 1876 she was certainly ahead of her time. I do not remember when she explained to me about sex in the beginning because I was too young to notice. These things are easier in a large family, with new babies arriving at intervals and their elders more or less interested in the process according to their age. My sister Eily was born when I was four. I knew that the baby that was coming was inside my mother where the bulge was, because I was told when I went for my morning cuddle in my mother's bed before she got up, that if I put my head on the bulge I might perhaps even be able to hear its heart beating, because it was alive already. I knew my father had had the baby to start with and given it to her, because he loved her and she wanted one, by putting part of himself right inside her (showing me on my own plump little anatomy just where) and the baby, so small, like a seed, you couldn't even know it was going to be a baby yet, had gone from him to her, where there was a place made just ready for it to grow in. It was quite comfy there while it got bigger and bigger, like 'having a cuddle all the time' (perhaps I remember that line from hearing her explain it to Eily, who was then six, and not long before Anne was born), until it got bored and wanted to come out, when there'd be room to grow as big as it liked.

I remember being furiously angry one day when Eily was due, and screaming with rage, shaking the little white gate on the nursery landing at the top of the stairs, because I'd been told that with any luck the baby might be born that day, and everyone had disappeared and I suspected them of having the baby to play with before I did. All the children in the house used to watch the new baby being fed, including my brother, who was ten. She was born in December, so it must have been the school holidays.

By the time Eily was of an age to run about and grab my toys, apparently I decided that it was time we had a new baby who would be less obstreperous, and my mother told me later that I asked my father to give her another one, implying that his last gift of the kind had not proved an unqualified success. She explained that every time he loved her so much he wanted to put the extra-kind bit of himself right inside her he couldn't always give her a baby even if they both wanted one: it depended on whether God thought we should all have another one yet. 'I realised,' she said, 'that you hadn't got the whole idea the first time, and I was more careful with Eily and Anne when they were small to give them one bit of information at a time.' It was six years, and my mother was forty-two, before Anne arrived, and I had probably given up hoping and lost interest. But I must have filed the information away, because I am told that I thanked my father for persuading God to let him provide the baby, when I knew it was coming, and that I only hoped it would be a boy, as Brendan, then sixteen, 'didn't count'.

I went to boarding school when I was six. My menstrual periods started when I was eleven, and that did startle the nuns. They made soothing noises and whisked me into bed, which I thought idiotic: my mother had expressly told me, sometime or other, that it wasn't being ill when you started to have 'periods', it was just 'beginning to be a woman', and you always had them until you were going to have a baby, when the baby would need you to have all your blood to help it grow.

I was left, champing with boredom, until my mother, for whom they had telephoned, arrived. She was (she told me later) furious with the nuns for letting there be such a fuss: the child was admittedly very young, but she had been properly prepared and fuss about any aspect of sex was bad for children. She refused to come and see me in the Infirmary as if I were ill, and they were to let me get up at once and come down and see her in the ordinary way. She then simply said wasn't it lucky that it hadn't been a Sunday or Thursday when parents were normally allowed, so that I had an extra visit.

I remember all that myself, but the earlier things that I had forgotten I think she told me when I was older so that I would bring up my own children on the same principle: you are never too young to learn anything, and you may easily be too old. When I was thirteen or so, my contemporaries used to get into corners and whisper about their developing breasts and their theories. One said that 'it must be something like cats', because she had come upon some kittens being born in the stables at home when she was little and had been whisked away and told it was nasty and she was to forget about it. I must have been overheard illuminating the other children because I was sent for by the Mistress General (head-mistress), who told me that my mother was a very sensible person who explained things, but some mothers didn't like their children to know things till later; so I must just tell her if any of them seemed to be puzzled and guessing, and she would ask their mothers to explain: it was a thing for mothers to do.

I never did have any children of my own to bring up on my mother's principles, but I was glad of her advice when I was living in Rome and a friend with a twelve-year-old daughter begged me to 'explain the facts of life' to the child: 'It's so embarrassing for a mother,' she said. She made dreadfully elaborate preparations so that it should all seem quite casual (as I had told her not to make a fuss), dreaming up some improbable reason why she and her husband had to go away for a week-end without the child, and saying I had invited her to stay in my flat. To my mind the little girl was already much too old to have things infiltrated into her mind gradually and naturally by my mother's methods, which presupposed that one was dealing with a tot; but I remembered her showing me a beautiful drawing in a book of a baby in the womb, and a lot of anatomical studies which I had found fascinating. The drawings had looked so pretty to the child I had been, but who could they have been by?

I shot round to the studio of an artist friend: yes, here was a book of Leonardo da Vinci's studies, and there was the enchanting unborn baby, and there were the beautiful male and female anatomies. I took the book home, and left it lying about open at the appropriate page. As soon as the little girl lighted on it I sat down by her: weren't the drawings lovely? I pass the tip on to mothers in the same predicament. Very soon I was secretly laughing, and we were looking at the other drawings in the book. On the Monday morning when she came to collect her daughter, my friend sent her out on some errand and asked me anxiously if if I'd managed all right.

'My dear,' I said, 'the child's at school at the French Lycée. There is nothing, but *nothing*, she didn't know about "life" already.'

There were two things that my mother forgot to 'infiltrate' into my mind. When I was fourteen, and beginning to be mad about the theatre and to read every play I could lay my hands on, we were discussing Ibsen one day when she and I were having lunch alone together. I said that *Hedda Gabler* was terrific, but *The Doll's House* was a bore, with that soppy young man going on about 'Give me the moon, mother,' for no earthly reason.

'Oh lord,' said my mother, 'don't tell me I forgot to explain about hereditary syphilis?' She proceeded to, telling me also how she had once met a woman in a train, obviously in a state of great strain, and had got her talking: she had found that her child had the disease, like the young man in the Ibsen play, and she was going to the cemetery where her husband was buried 'to spit on his grave'. I thought the whole thing was revolting and terrible and burst into tears.

'There you are,' said my mother, 'you're too old and it's a shock.' The parlourmaid came in to clear the table as I wept, and my mother went on soothing me, as she did so telling me about the sensible police inspections of brothels in France which there ought to be everywhere 'because there'll always be brothels' and how there was now a cure for syphilis anyhow and people should always go to a doctor at once. When I had cheered up, she said, 'Now, is there anything else I've forgotten to tell you, for goodness sake?' How could I tell? 'I know,' she said, 'homosexuality—have I explained to you about that?' I shook my head, and she said, 'It used to happen in monasteries in the Middle Ages, and in the trenches in the War because there weren't any women,' and went on to explain. My mind, such as it is, has always worked almost entirely in visual images, and for years the word homosexual called up a picture of a young man with a tonsure, a cowl and a scapular, but otherwise dressed as an officer in the First World War.

What my mother's own sex education as a child had been I have no idea, but I suspect that it had been acquired haphazardly from her father. Her mother, after all, had been born in the eighteen-fifties, when babies were found under gooseberry bushes. But her father had never had any idea that a child was in any way different from an adult except in the matter of size, and evidently talked to her as one; and he did have such an abiding interest in anatomy.

Another aspect of the Facts of Life I learned not so much at my mother's knee but, by her guidance, at Aunt Patty's. If Patty Dillon had been an aunt at all she would have been a great-aunt, but she was in fact only an infinitely remote cousin. She was the much-younger sister of Adda Dillon, who had helped their guardian uncle to bring up my father's sisters. Granny Dilly had been my godmother and when she died when I was eight or so Aunt Patty considered she had inherited the responsibility not so much of my spiritual welfare as of godmotherly birthday and Christmas presents, in return for which it seemed reasonable that I should be the one sent to see if she wanted anything, such as a library book changed or some silk matched at Harrods. I became devoted to her and, my little commissions for her done, would sit for hours coaxing out of her stories about the middle of the last century in France, and about all the men in the portraits and photographs that covered every spare inch of space in her drawing-room. They might have been considered by many an odd diet for a convent-bred little girl of the period, but my mother smiled affectionately over those I recounted at home and told me how lucky I was to know so old a lady with so wonderful a memory.

Orphaned in Ireland at three years old Aunt Patty had been sent to the nearest relation with any money, a General Charles Dillon in the French Service. He in turn, being a bachelor, had dumped her on friends, the Kinnemonts in Touraine, and that was a story in itself. As a young subaltern he had struck up a friendship with a brother officer, the Marquis de Kinnemont, descendant (as Dillon was from the Wild Geese) of a Scottish archer of Louis XI's called Kinmont, and immensely proud of his mercenary ancestry. When Dillon fell in love with the daughter of a landowner in the vicinity of their depôt, having no relative to do the job for him he asked Kinnemont to make the necessary arrangements for the match with her father—this must have been shortly after the end of the Napoleonic wars. The father declined to allow a young man with nothing but his military prospects (of which Kinnemont spoke glowingly) to propose to his daughter, but assured the young Marquis that he would look favourably on any approach he cared to make on his own behalf. Kinnemont had seen the girl, who was a considerable heiress with land not far from his own estates, and he went back to his principal: Dillon hadn't a hope in hell himself, he told him, so had he any objection to Kinnemont following up the father's suggestion? Dillon was realist enough to accept the situation, but romantic enough to remain in love with the new Marquise de Kinnemont, for the rest of his life, while continuing the good friend of her husband.

Thus into the Kinnemont ménage, in their town house in Tours, Patty arrived as a tot, and watched as she grew older the Marquise growing sadder, and thinner, and more and more of a recluse, her hair and teeth falling out while she was still quite young, never leaving her own rooms and hardly ever receiving guests, lavishing affection on Charles Dillon's little ward and living for such visits as his military career allowed. Kinnemont was devoted to Patty too, and she adored him. Soon he began to take her every summer on his annual tour of his estates. Mme de Kinnemont would put into the lattice of red tapes in the domed top of Patty's trunk a note addressed to 'The Housekeeper' at the château in Touraine about any small ailment of Patty's that needed attention; and when Kinnemont and Patty moved on the 'Housekeeper' there would address another note of such advice to 'The Housekeeper' at the villa above Nice to which they always went next. In fact the first lady was the daughter of Kinnemont's nurse, whom he had seduced when they were both sixteen, and the second had been the wife of another officer of his regiment, his liaison with whom had led to his leaving the service and her leaving her husband. A third lady lived on his forest property near Le Mans; a fourth, a retired actress, in a beautiful little house on some farmland of his near Fontainebleau. There were eventually seven such ladies, all of whom Patty visited with Kinnemont except, always, his current mistress who lived in his flat in Paris and was visited by him constantly at other times until she graduated to a home on one of his other properties and became part of the summer tour. They all continued to love Kinnemont and live for his visits and to adore and spoil Patty outrageously. The euphemism was always kept up that the ladies

elsewhere were simply the housekeepers at their respective properties, and they were never talked about. Patty loved them all,
doted on Kinnemont, and had a wonderful time everywhere.

It was certainly a childhood as different from my mother's as
hers was from mine, and stories about it were, equally certainly,
broadening to the mind.

When Patty was eighteen her official guardian Charles Dillon
introduced to her in Paris a young cousin of theirs who had
looked him up on arrival there on holiday, a medical student from
Dublin, Jimmy Dillon. The young people of course fell in love.
Kinnemont was outraged—a medical student, indeed, to marry
his exquisite Patty? Unthinkable. That Mme de Kinnemont,
victim of an arranged marriage, should back the love match was
predictable; but what was surely remarkable was that, relying
on their support, she should have written to the first five of those
ladies, whose names she knew perfectly well, including the nurse's
daughter from the château who was perhaps Patty's favourite,
inviting them to Tours for a sort of family council, to support
her against her husband on behalf of Patty's love. More remarkable still, all five came (though Kinnemont fled to Paris),
all got along admirably, but all banded together against the folly
of a love match when Kinnemont was prepared to dower her for
one so much better. Alas, while the Marquise planned an elope-
ment for her, Patty got a telegram from Dublin: Jimmy had got
an infected hand from an accident in the operating theatre; and
three days later he died.

Apart from the other joys of the summer tours, each of the
ladies had passionately differing views on how Patty should be
dressed, and though she travelled from house to house in the
clothes provided by the Marquise, in each was kept for her a
deliciously distinctive wardrobe added to on each visit, which
gave her a delight in clothes and a taste that remained exquisite

into her nineties. My mother laughed when I repeated to her Aunt Patty's story of her wardrobes, and recalled how she herself, with a blind mother, had been dressed when she was little according to her father' dictates: light colours were cool and had to be worn in summer, dark dresses were warm and *de rigueur* for winter; otherwise anything that covered her decently was fine. She told me to pay great attention to Patty's opinions on my own clothes, for she feared that she herself had never developed such taste.

After months of deep distress, loving care from the Marquise, and frenzied efforts by Kinnemont to line up an acceptable husband, Patty left for London and a part-time job as a governess that would enable her to work on the research for a historical novel (subsequently published) called *Earl or Chieftain*, set in Ireland in the reign of Elizabeth. Every morning her employer, on his way to his office in the City, dropped Patty off at the British Museum Reading Room, placing a bunch of violets on her desk before he left her. One day when he was kept at home by a cold, a snuffy old gentleman who always sat at a neighbouring desk and distracted Patty by his coughing and nose-blowing, suddenly left soon after she arrived, returning with a bunch of violets which he laid on her desk with a note: 'Lest the Flower of the Reading Room should miss the company of her sisters.' Such was the sort of effect that Patty seems always to have had; yet she never married.

She never wrote another book, either, but she certainly exercised her gift for story-telling on me, when I asked her about the portraits and photographs on her walls and tables. There was one miniature by the fireplace with which I fell in love at an early age, an ancestor of hers in the 18th century in Ireland who had planned to elope, as she had done. He had told his father that he was running a horse at some distant races next day and asked to borrow the family chaplain to bless it before it was taken there. When they reached the stables he locked the door, opened a corn bin and produced his girl, and with two grooms as witnesses forced the chaplain at pistol-point to marry them; he then rode off with the bride for the coast, having padlocked the chaplain in the corn bin with instructions to the grooms not to let him out till the happy couple were well on their way to France. He died young, in France in a duel over his wife's favours, fought on a table top with his wife forced to sit and watch. My next love was a beautiful young Russian prince in a photograph with a silver frame and a devoted inscription, whom she had befriended in exile in London after the Students' Revolt in 1905—his story was equally colourful; and there were many more.

Even in her nineties she was the most exquisitely and entirely feminine creature I have ever known. When an unexploded bomb fell in 1941 on the convent in Brompton Square where she then had rooms, and the residents were evacuated, Aunt Patty, protesting politely that she could easily walk, was carried down on a stretcher by, she told me afterwards, 'two such handsome young men from the Rescue Service'. She was only upset because she had been in bed at the time (no nonsense about going to shelters for her!) wearing her warmest but least attractive nightgown, and I had only recently bought her an especially alluring one from Harrods, covered with lace to her specifications.

I once asked her how, in spite of losing Jimmy, she had managed never to marry in all her years. She looked with a reminiscent smile round the room. 'With so many enchanting men in the world,' she said, 'it seemed a pity to settle for just one.'

Music
in the Home

When I left Oxford I decided to be the first female Prime
Minister in England. It seemed a reasonable ambition, since I
had taken a good degree that included Economics. In my last
term but one, my Economics tutor, a woman of considerable
perception, had written a report to my college tutor: 'Economic
Theory. Miss Boland. Miss Boland does not understand Economic
Theory.' I got a β++ in Economic Theory in my finals. If
I could fool so many of the examiners so much of the time, I
was clearly cut out for politics. The only drawback was that my
voice would not carry to the third row of a church hall; so my
mother arranged for me to go for an audition to the great Elsie
Fogarty, the leading voice authority of the day. Miss Fogarty
listened to me for a moment, and then struck a note on the
piano.

'Pitch it there,' she said.
'I'm sorry, I can't sing,' said I.
'Just *say* a word, but pitch it—there—'
'Hullo,' I said hopelessly.
'Oh dear. Try this—there—'
'Hullo.'

Miss Fogarty looked at me thoughtfully. 'Turn away a moment.
Now, which of these notes is the higher—one, or two?'

So far as I was concerned she might have hit the top note and the bottom of the entire keyboard (and I gather she practically did). Well, there was a fifty-fifty chance.

'Two,' I said.

'Good God!' She frowned thoughtfully, then 'Boland!' she exclaimed, 'of course! Do you know, I've only found one other human being in my entire life as completely, as wonderfully tone deaf as you are, and that was your mother.' She had taught her when she first married, and was going to have to make speeches in my father's constituency, even if only of the bazaar-opening type. 'Don't worry, my dear. I remember having to work out a method of teaching pitch without music for her, and she could fill the Albert Hall without a microphone by the time we'd finished. I kept my notes of the case somewhere, I was so proud of it. I'll dig them out.'

I learned no music at my mother's knee.

My father on the other hand, had, I was told, a charming light tenor. He certainly had a delightful speaking voice. He could even play the piano well enough for us to dance jigs and reels to. He tried to teach me to play 'Seated one day at the organ' with one hand. As he said, the beginning was easy enough: you simply hit the first note about ten times. I enjoyed that, and could even remember the notes for 'weary and ill at ease', but the rest defeated me. At school we had a great deal of music. Early on, the peculiar noises I made at singing classes were detected and I was given private coaching (almost equally ineffectual) in mathematics instead. There were recitals by professional pianists or violinists every Thursday afternoon. We wore white gloves for such formal occasions, and these concerts reduced the fingertips to shreds as I bit them and rubbed them in nervous agitation. Finally, at a recital entirely of Beethoven (whose tinkling and crashing were the worst of all), I suddenly jumped up and screamed: 'Stop it! Stop!' and rushed from the hall; and thereafter my mother persuaded the nuns to let me off the torture which musical people are so curiously unable to recognise as such. I understand that nowadays it has been discovered how to teach tone-deaf children to sing. I cannot conceive how it can give them any pleasure, and there are far too many people who can, and do, alas, sing already. It is all Shakespeare's fault, saying that the likes of me were fit for treasons, stratagems and spoils. Yet as always he was right, and I may well be discovered one day creeping like a serpent on my belly cutting the wires that lead to loud speakers in public places. I have already learned how to do it without electrocuting myself...

Religion

—————⊃∘◐∘⊂—————

Both my parents were deeply religious.

My father's brand of Catholicism was the taken-for-granted kind of the good born Catholic, given an intellectual bent by the fact that Cardinal Newman had been his headmaster at school and an additional impetus, when, in late middle age, the Irish cause fell to pieces in his hands and he was a man who had to have a cause. He took over the running of a non-profit making (it had to be that) publishing organisation, the Catholic Truth Society, and devoted the rest of his life to it. In his eighties he could still be seen proof-reading a new translation of the Bible (in very small print, without glasses) with Homer at his elbow for relaxation (as he feared he was forgetting his Greek). When a new Papal Encyclical came out, the whole family used to be coralled to help: my father with the Latin text, my mother with the official Italian translation, one of us reading aloud the English translation he was publishing, with him and my mother querying the wording of it from the sense of their texts, and the rest of us proof-reading, one inserting their queries for the translator and the others who were old enough each supposed to spot any typographical errors the others missed. I hated this, and soon managed to opt out on the grounds , all too true, that my own spelling was unreliable anyway.

I never heard my father talk about religion as such. The only prayer book I ever saw him use, apart from a Latin missal, was one in Irish that had belonged to Daniel O'Connel ('the Liberator'), which he used, I think, lest he should forget his Irish. He went to the seven o'clock Mass every day of his life, always jogging there and back to keep fit—but properly dressed and wearing a hat and carrying gloves, of course.

My mother's religion was quite different, if just the same. It was summed up, I think, in her pleasure in a psalm used at the beginning of Mass: 'I will go up unto the altar of God,' says the priest; 'Of God who giveth joy to my youth,' says the acolyte. 'I have loved, O Lord,' she would quote, 'the beauty of thy house, and the place where thy glory dwelleth.' Religion for her meant beauty, beauty of the ritual, of Church architecture, of sculpture, of paintings. Religion meant Christendom, and the beauty of the idea of it (and back we go, of course, to that childhood of hers, wandering about the churches and galleries of Europe). Christendom implied Catholicism: the Reformation had spoilt it, not for her but for the Protestants: 'How can they understand or enjoy it, poor dears?' The darker aspects of church history didn't trouble her at all. When I asked her about the Borgia popes, for instance, she said 'Well they were men, of course. And men of their time, at that. You aren't mixing up infallibility with impeccability, are you?' And it was she who showed me pictures of the shields with the Borgia coat of arms round the bases of the pillars round the high altar in St Peter's . Above each shield is carved the face of the same woman, and the shields are shaped like her torso, with the three Borgia bees placed for, as it might be, her nipples and her navel. The first face is expressionless, and the first shield flat. In the second carving the face is troubled and the shield swollen; in the third the shield looks nine months pregnant, the face is contorted and the mouth open in a soundless scream. In the fourth the shield is flat again, and the face of the woman replaced by that of a smiling baby. The baldachino that the pillars support was erected by Alexander VI (Borgia) in thanksgiving for the successful outcome of a difficult pregnancy of his mistress. When I first went to live in Rome myself during the pontificate of Pius XI (Pacelli), I remembered another story of hers (to stress the difference between infallibility and impeccability): there was once, in the middle ages, a French merchant who had a friend in Paris who was a Jew who was thinking of becoming a Christian. The latter had to go to Rome on business, and the former thought that, alas, that would be the end of his hopes for his friend's conversion. But the Jew came back a Christian in spite of all. 'Any church,' he said, 'that can survive so long with men like that at the head of it must have God on its side.'

Music in church was a torment to her except plainsong, which was 'natural', and it was such a pity that the best ritual occasions were always ruined by organists and choirmasters who chose 'to make all that terrible noise'. She told me a story she had heard in Avignon: the chapel in the Palace of the Popes, built when they were in exile from Rome, had such bad acoustics that one note of plainsong was still echoing when the next was sung: so they made the best of a bad job and developed polyphonic music.

Of piety in the home we had not too much, considering how religious our parents were. My mother considered we had perhaps rather too much of it compulsorily at our Convent school. Westminster Cathedral was our parish church. My mother likened the exterior to 'three gasometers and a factory chimney', but she liked the interior, with people going so busily about their devotions 'like Basle railway station'. Of our own volition we would get up at dawn on Easter Saturday morning to enjoy the romantic ritual of the Easter Fire lit on the steps outside, and carried by the Paschal Candle up the nave, in a ceremony that my mother was convinced that Shakespeare must have enjoyed in his Catholic boyhood. The speech 'On such a night as this' in the Merchant of Venice is a palpable echo of the chant 'Haec nox est', only instead of 'This is the night in which . . .' Abraham led forth the children of Israel, and so on, Lorenzo turns it to such parallels as the night on which Leander swam the Hellespont to join his love, and Lorenzo stole forth his Jessica from out of the house of Shylock the Jew.

Punishment, recognisable as such, in our house there was none. The impression given was that if you were tiresome people wouldn't stop loving you, of course, but would find it very difficult not to. I myself had the advantage (or otherwise?) of the fact that the three older children had apparently been born practically without original sin: they actually preferred to be good; and anyone could see that they were entirely lovable. I redressed the balance with at least three times more tendency to be hell to live with than the average child. Whenever this became too apparent I was told I must be overtired, or sickening for something, and had better go to bed. 'But bed tires me,' I protested. 'That's just because you do run up and down it so,' said my mother. 'We'll draw the window curtains, and you just go nicely to sleep and you'll be better in no time. I'll come up and see how you are at teatime.' I really did grow up thinking that being naughty meant that you were ill, but that I seemed to have been born with a debility in this direction that my elders didn't suffer from, which was hard luck. I was not naturally logically-minded, or of course I might simply have said: 'If I'm ill it's not my fault. I just can't help doing what I want to.' I thought instead that if I wanted to be lovable I had better grow out of it. I don't know what modern psychologists would make of this method but surely it was better than the 'spare the rod and spoil the child' principle still current in most homes at that time.

In some respects it was very much easier to bring up children in those days in that religious setting than it is now. That it was wrong to steal, for instance, was so much an opinion in the ambient air that I cannot imagine gangs of infant shoplifters would have been prevalent even if supermarkets had been invented. As for sexual morality, my mother felt that there was too much emphasis in our time on sanctions, for girls on 'If you sleep with a man you aren't married to you might have an illegitimate baby', and for boys on 'If you are promiscuous you'll probably pick up V.D.'. Her own line was: 'The capacity for love, as opposed to desire, is what makes you human. If you have sexual relations without love you are behaving like an animal, and if you fall for a man you can't marry you're wasting love and you're a goose. Real love is forever.' She felt that the nuns at school didn't instil a sense of proportion: 'There really is a difference between "Thou shalt not run in the corridors, or whistle, or sit with thy legs crossed" and "Thou shalt not covet thy neighbour's husband",' she said. It was easy enough for her, mind you: she was no goose. If there had been the gaiety of romance in the friendships of her later girlhood, the man she loved was the man she married, and their love was indeed forever.

For the more mystical aspects of religion neither of my parents had, I fancy, any gift at all, though they had an intellectual grasp of them and of their benefits without the temperamental equipment for their enjoyment, unless love and joy themselves are mystical gifts. 'This is the day that the Lord has made,' my mother arranged to have engraved on her tombstone, 'let us rejoice and be glad therein.'

High Romance

Christmas in Nuremburg—or Naples—or Lisbon; Easter in Paris—or Florence—or Seville; the Summer in Padua—on the Loire—or in Vienna—and then a sudden trip to Australia, exchanging a term or so at Roehampton for the Melbourne school of the same order; my mother had no abiding place, and she once told me that she found her permanence in time and not in space. The 15th century, or the 16th, or the 18th were each the same wherever you were, and she could find the same sort of things of any period in a new town as she had known in the last, and that gave a sense of the known, with differences that then became fascinating. She developed a passion for history and for an awareness of periods for this reason, because in her awareness of the past around her she could always be at home. She wanted us to have above all the security of roots; but it seemed sad that we couldn't then have the other thing, the fascination of new places and the awareness of European culture which she felt could only come from living all over Europe.

Our financial position became very different from what hers had been as a child. Like 'Gran's husband', my father never earned any money. It would ruin the British Parliamentary System, he felt, if payment were ever introduced: it would turn membership into a profession instead of a vocation for people like himself who believed in a cause. But after the 1914–18 War money began not to

have the value it used to have, and by the 'twenties when the Irish
Party ceased to exist, he was middle-aged, without a profession,
except at the Bar, at which it was too late to begin to practise, and
with no notion how one began to find another. At the same time
my mother's money from Australian property had been eroded
by mysterious things like Bank Crashes. It didn't matter, there
was still plenty to live on: but constant jaunts about the Continent
for six children were out of the question.

So we learned to travel in time to take us away from home, as
my mother had done for such a different reason.

One of our best games with her we called 'Place for a Murder'.
It derived from a line of Robert Louis Stevenson's about how
'some places cry out for murder'. Not that there always had to be
one. Any ancient building, or better still a street of them, would
serve. In a way it was an extension of 'Going for a Walk in a
Picture', but more dramatic. You said what kind of thing might
have happened in such a place at the time the sight of it
evoked. You filled it with the right kind of people doing the
right kind of things, and wearing the right kind of clothes, and
you developed the action of the story. It was the perfect way to
make tourism exciting. I have done murder most foul ('which
in the best it is', as my mother frequently pointed out in view of
our apparent lust for blood) in every cathedral I visited, inter-
rupted weddings and broken up funerals, and had rival sculptors
and architects and window designers hurl each other to the ground
from scaffoldings; I have had Black Masses celebrated in crypts,
and body-snatchers open graves in cemeteries. ('Can't we come
back by moonlight? You could see so much better to imagine
by!') The things we saw going on in the old Inns of Court,
particularly the Temple! The clothes and the characters and the
sort of story had to fit the setting: you could choose a period later
than the actual buildings, but not one earlier. You could not

exactly win such a game, it was a joint evocation; Eily was best at historical accuracy: she took a very good degree in history at Oxford later; Maureen was best at providing the clothes and the furniture; I provided most of the drama and all the blood.

There were good Dickensian-type settings in London, of course, particularly along the river, and Austenian and Trollopian settings in provincial towns, but abroad was better than England for the game whenever we did go (except in Wissant in the summer, which was strictly here-and-now); in Bruges and Ghent and Brussels on one trip Maureen and I played it endlessly. When I was quite old, eighteen, my mother and I were (irresistibly even if laughingly) playing it in an arcaded street in Anneçy, when we noticed two solemn English tourists behind listening avidly: where had we come upon this story, they asked—it wasn't in their guide book. I was dreadfully embarrassed, but my mother glibly provided the title and authour of a non-existent book in French which she feared was out of print. 'With any luck they'll pass it on,' she said as we hurried away. 'That's how legends start.'

She can have had no-one to play such time games with herself when she was young, and must have dreamed them on her own; and not wandered about dreaming them either, for a brisk walk the shortest way to the church, gallery or museum was all that was permitted to a young girl alone. Her father often took her sight-seeing, but does not sound the kind of man to waste time on flights of fancy when there were other things to press on and see; and her mother, growing ever blinder, would not have enjoyed the idea either.

As she grew older, however, company of her own age there inevitably was and less need to escape into times past to find a permanence of reality—or romance. She always told me she was never beautiful, but the photographs and one painting that I have of her show a charming, lively face, hazel eyes that were almost green, and the kind of fair hair that darkens a little in each photograph. She was below average height (though both her parents were immensely tall), and very slim. As she grew older she was always beautifully dressed. Her mother, worried by the fact that she couldn't see what it was 'right' to wear, put herself and her daughter in the hands of a fashionable dressmaker in Paris called Madame Manalt, and both were entirely dressed by her. If my mother showed any independent ideas, her mother, fearing they might be unsuitable, assured her that 'Manalt knows best what's worn, dear', and that was that. So charming and lively a girl as she must have been could not fail to attract attention, and attention, in spite of the difficulties, she began to get.

I have still a long gold chain that she left me in her will. It hung almost to the waist, but a watch was worn on the end of it and it was looped up and pinned over the breast. From it hung at intervals little objects, as from the charm bracelets of my own youth, and it was known among young girls as a 'scalp chain', because on it you hung little tokens given to you by admirers. From it among other things hung, set in filigree, a sixpence with the die flattened at the back and engraved 'Alton 1896' and a mother-of-pearl button with a little gold disc set in the middle engraved 'Alton 1897'. These were records of the year-and-one-month that she spent in Australia when she was eighteen. They were lucky charms found in the puddings of two successive Christmases spent at the station of friends called Hood, at Alton in Queensland. The charms had been taken from my mother, after she won them from the pudding, by Lionel, the young son of the house, set and engraved and given back to her—the second sent by post to find her in Europe. As a child, naturally, I wove romance out of everything on the scalp chain, particularly the quaint gifts of Lionel Hood. So much trouble to take over a sixpence, and to set an ordinary button in gold! He must, he absolutely had to, have loved her. Did he? My mother used to smile and say that Lionel was a dear, but that as for love . . . and she could never have married him, with her by now completely blind mother and heavily-drinking father to look after, anyway.

Then there was the Vicomte Armand de—was it Vaugelard or Vaugirard? I never saw it written down and it echoes unclearly in my memory, for I was entirely fascinated by his being a Vicomte. She and her parents had gone back to Paris from Australia, for her to spend a year at the finishing school of the nuns of the order where she had been educated; was the finishing of her education the reason or the excuse for the flight from Australia? Wouldn't Lionel Hood 'do'? Romantic though Lionel certainly was, I really preferred a Vicomte for my mother on the whole, with a name like something out of the French history and novels that I loved. If Armand gave her romantic presents they were not so indentifiable as Lionel's, or had not survived, but there were some brown old photographs which included him, tall for a Frenchman, and slender, but with a straw hat so tilted over his eyes that you could see nothing of his face but a smiling mouth. A Vicomte *was* a Vicomte, and to be French was far more romantic than to be Irish: *why* hadn't she married him?

'Perhaps I was thinking of you,' she said. 'If I'd married Armand instead of Daddy you'd never have been born—or Honor, or Brendan, or Maureen, or Eily, or Anne either.' I remember that she said each name with a pause between, to give me time to imagine a world without them; and of course if she had been a Vicomtesse without me there to admire the fact, there would have been very little point in the exercise anyway. I didn't think to ask if he had ever asked her, as of course any man who had the chance would have done so. Listening back on it now, she didn't say he hadn't.

Then there was Jack Smith. The name was a bit of a come down after Armand's—I think it must have been Vaugelard, and that the Vaugirard that haunts me too is simply the rue Vaugirard in Paris. But I had the feeling that Jack Smith was more fun. He was not, by the fading photographs, such a smart dresser, but was more of a sporting type. He was usually rowing a boat with his shirt sleeves rolled up, or carrying a tennis racquet, or in knicker-bockers and carrying an alpenstock, and his hat, if he wore one at all, was always on the back of his head. But then this was Switzer-land, not Paris—Teritet, Montreux, Vevey, Jack Smith kept turning up. And there he is in Venice, with the gondolier laugh-ing as Jack wields the pole. He looks as if he is doing it rather well; and he has tied a ribbon round his straw hat with the ends hanging down behind as a gondolier should. A ribbon borrowed from my mother's dress, what's more. Lionel Hood married, Armand de Vaugelard vanished, what happened to Jack Smith?

'He died,' said my mother. I lost interest.

Young people in hotels there were, if not children, and my mother was seeing plenty of them now. 'Never chase men when you grow up,' she told me, 'they can always tell when you do.' Convinced that with her parents to care for she could never marry herself, she sat on the sidelines and watched the hotel flirtations of various nationalities with detached amusement. 'Because I was out of the game and let everybody know it,' she said, 'the young men used to confide in me.' She said that Henry James's *Daisy Miller* gave a perfect picture of the travelling American girls of the period, shocking Europeans even of their own age with their lack of the inhibitions considered proper.

'Wasn't it sad,' I asked her, 'just to be a wallflower yourself?'

'A wallflower? Not I,' she said, and she smiled reminiscently.

She used to miss travelling very much, and frequently quoted a poem from (surprisingly) Thackeray:

(133)

Poor Mrs Gill is very ill and nothing will improve 'er
Unless she see the Tuileries and waddles round the Louvre.

'Never mind, when you're old enough we'll go to Florence.'
When she was about twenty-three she went with her mother
to Wiesbaden, for the famous Dr Pagenstecher to look at the
latter's eyes. Pagenstecher was much disapproved of by many
oculists in England, for he had been called in over their heads to
treat Queen Victoria, with whom he had had considerable
success, and twice he had been reported in *The Times* as having
died. He certainly survived into the nineteen-twenties, when I
was taken to him at the age of fourteen or so, an English consultant
having given me spectacles for my slight apparent astigmatism,
which my mother thought a pity. Pagenstecher, a darling old
man, removed the spectacles and treated me for a couple of
months with massage and exercises, after which the muscles
worked perfectly and, having kept up the exercises for a year, I
never needed glasses again till I got some for reading in my late
fifties. In the case of my grandmother the trouble was cataract,
the operation for which was then improperly understood and
seldom performed. She had been blind for years when Pagenstecher cured her with some chemical treatment. As the film over
her eyes began to clear, or perhaps shrivel away from the middle,
she said to my mother: 'It's exactly like the man said in the New
Testament: I see men like trees walking.' New horizons opened
for my mother, too.

It was when she and I were staying at the Rose Hotel in
Wiesbaden for my treatment that she told me about her real
love story, for it was there, in a sense, that it had begun.

She had looked one day in the hotel register to discover the
names of two girls of about her own age who attracted her, who
were travelling with an older lady. They were the Misses Nancy

and Mary Boland and Miss Dillon. The name Boland meant nothing to her, but that of Dillon was famous in Irish history. She
was at the time teaching herself Irish, and here was a heaven-
sent opportunity to clear up a point in her grammar. She had
never been in Ireland, and could not understand what was meant
by a certain combination of letters being pronounced 'in one and
a half syllables, as in "elm" '. She approached the group in the
lounge ('over there, in that corner') and appealed to Miss Dillon
to help, showing the grammar. Miss Dillon explained apolo-
getically that only the country people of the South and West
spoke Irish nowadays and a few scholars, but the girls were
looking at the grammar and laughed.

'With a brogue,' said one, 'elm is pronounced ellum!'

My mother, who had been trying it with a French e mute
on the end, which hadn't helped, was delighted. The girls were
vastly amused by her efforts, and said that she should meet their
brother Patrick, who had learned Irish and was great at it. She
begged them to send him other queries, and they promised to do
so, and they became great friends. Their cousin Miss Dillon was
the ideal chaperone, and with her in tow they could wander about
freely in the town and drive as far as Bingen on the Rhine together. Their brother sent answers to the queries and my mother
gave them more to send to him, and when her mother, seeing
well, decided to leave for London, she was quite sad to part with
them and they exchanged addresses.

They looked in on Paris on the way, to get some clothes—
after all, she would now be able to see them. My grandmother
had no sense of geography, and always thought they should look
in on Paris on the way anywhere, including, my mother swore, on
the way from Naples to Rome. Madame Manalt was worried about
my mother: a client who had not found a husband by the age of
twenty-three was a slur on her dressmaking. She announced that

she would make her '*une robe de conquête*'.

'Gran's husband' had joined them in London and they had taken a flat in Queen Anne's mansions, overlooking St James's Park, but my mother was alone in the sitting-room one day when the very young page brought her the card of a Mr John Boland, showing him in at the same time. My mother was unable to escape. She was by no means wearing the '*robe de conquête*' (white, with dark red bows), but an old skirt and a hideous striped flannel blouse. What is more she was lying on the sofa with a hot water bottle, nursing a cold. She shoved the bottle under a pillow, upon which Mr Boland incontinently sat—though he should have known better than to sit on a sofa next to a young woman on first meeting her, when there was plenty of other chairs in the room. However, she asked after his sisters and said it was so kind of his brother Patrick to answer all her queries. Mr Boland explained that indeed Patrick was the great Irish scholar of the family but a shocking correspondent, and that he was himself the brother that had answered, as he had some Irish himself and the queries had not been difficult.

Mr Boland explained that he was a Member of Parliament, representing South Kerry. He invited my mother and her parents to tea on the Terrace of the House, to this, and to that, and to the other. He was six foot two, with an Irishman's bright blue eyes and long upper lip separated by a classically perfect Roman nose. He was quiet, gentle, entirely good, and a hundred per cent, twenty-four hours a day fanatic.

My mother once showed me her diary of the year in which she became twenty-four. For several weeks, always in the mornings except at the weekends (for the House was sitting), there was entry after entry that read 'with Father and Mr Boland to the Academy', 'with Mother and Mr Boland to walk in the Park'. At weekends it was 'with Violet and Mr Boland to the Star and

Garter at Richmond then on to Henley to watch rowing'. Violet was a friend of her own age, but she was married and therefore a suitable chaperone. One Friday it read 'with Mother to tea with Mr Boland on the Terrace'. Then there was a gap of four days in the diary, and then 'with Mother and John to . . .' I forget where.

'I've always wished he'd proposed that day on the Terrace. It would have been so much more romantic. As it was we went on the river next day with Violet and her husband, to Eel Pie Island.' I agreed that Eel Pie Island did not sound romantic at all, and asked what eel pies were like; but gathered that there hadn't been any in living memory. Perhaps it was pretty. He had of course asked her father's permission to propose to her. Even when she was engaged to him, my mother could not visit John's chambers at 12 King's Bench Walk, in the Temple, without a chaperone.

They were married that year and lived happily ever after till my mother died in 1937. Then my father simply went to bed. He saw nothing to get up for. For months he stayed there, with a nurse because we were frightened, but he was not ill. His manners were too good to refuse to eat when he saw that it distressed us, and eventually his excellent physique defeated him: all that tennis, all those cold baths every morning, all that walking up and down Kerry hills, all that walking always everywhere when other people sat in cars. His body got up, and lived, in a way, for another twenty years.

TAILPIECE

It is said that we never really grow up till we can recognise that our parents were no better and no worse than other people's. Ah, well, at my age it is too late to bother to try. Mine gave me a singularly happy childhood. Alas, all the best writers, especially nowadays, have had miserable childhoods. Pray forgive me, it is too late for me to do anything about that either.